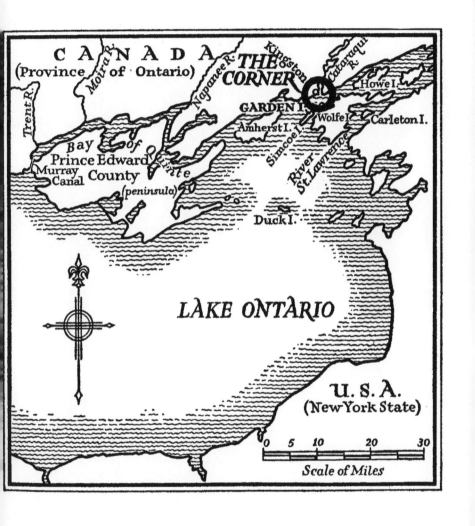

CANADA
(Province of Ontario)

Trent R.

Moira R.

Napanee R.

Kingston

THE CORNER

Cataraqui R.

Howe I.

GARDEN I.

Wolfe I.

Carleton I.

Amherst I.

Simcoe I.

Bay of Prince Edward County (peninsula)

Murray Canal

River St. Lawrence

Duck I.

LAKE ONTARIO

U.S.A.
(New York State)

0   5   10   20   30

Scale of Miles

A CORNER OF EMPIRE

A CORNER OF EMPIRE

The Old Ontario Strand

by

T. R. GLOVER

and

D. D. CALVIN

CAMBRIDGE
AT THE UNIVERSITY PRESS
1937

CAMBRIDGE
UNIVERSITY PRESS

University Printing House, Cambridge CB2 8BS, United Kingdom

Published in the United States of America by Cambridge University Press, New York

Cambridge University Press is part of the University of Cambridge.

It furthers the University's mission by disseminating knowledge in the pursuit of education, learning and research at the highest international levels of excellence.

www.cambridge.org
Information on this title: www.cambridge.org/9781107425651

© Cambridge University Press 1937

First published 1937
First paperback edition 2014

A catalogue record for this publication is available from the British Library

ISBN 978-1-107-42565-1 Paperback

PREFACE

A Corner of Empire—for three Empires fought to control
the place, the gateway of the West, a key position for the
fur trade, and, all along, vital for the future of Upper Canada
and of the great North West beyond. When at last war with
Frenchman and American was over, here rose the town, the
King's Town, of the United Empire Loyalists; here was for
sixty years the centre of a new trade, till there were no longer
forests to fell, and men could build rafts no more; and here
for nearly a century has stood a University "on the old
Ontario strand". All this for all the world; and for the
authors, memories of friendship and happiness, and the
"rememberable things" that Nature speaks, in the beauty
of a great lake and a great river, open water and open sky.

T. R. G.
D. D. C.

Dominion Day, 1937

CONTENTS

For readers who are worried about disentangling any strands of autobiography, let it be said that chapters I, II and VIII are in the main the work of T. R. G., and chapters III, IV, V and VI of D. D. C., while both had a hand in chapter VII.

ILLUSTRATIONS

PLATES

The engravings reproduced in plates I–V are from drawings made by W. H. Bartlett (1809–1854). Many volumes of his pictures were issued by George Virtue, a noted London publisher. His *American Scenery* (1840, two volumes) and *Canadian Scenery* (1842, two volumes) are still "sought" by book-collectors. One or two minor inaccuracies may be found in the pictures; but most readers will find a peculiar charm in these pictures of a hundred years ago, which give, in their general effect, as no others do, a vivid sense of the beauty of our familiar scenes.

Plates VI–IX are from original photographs by D. D. and C. C. Calvin, and Plate X from a painting by J. D. Kelly, based on photographs supplied by D. D. C., and here reproduced by courtesy of Rolph-Clark-Stone Ltd., Toronto, whose property it is.

The portrait of G. M. Grant is by Notman and Sons, Montreal.

Chapter I

THE KEY OF EMPIRE

§ 1. THE THEME

A quiet old town on the Great Lake, and unprogressive—to the stranger who races through it in his car for some other destination it may seem not unlike the other small towns through which he dashes. There is indeed a certain outward likeness, cultivated by such as love to "keep in line"—let us have (is their feeling) streets of "beautiful homes", as the Americans call them, lined by well-grown shade-trees and trim lawns without a fence; and then at least one street full of hustling modernity, shoe-parlours, dry goods stores, cinemas, telephone poles, and strings of automobiles, and general tawdriness; add a huge modern school or two, sometimes with 1880 written in every dull line of them. Yes, alas! we have all that; but we have something more—an unusual beauty of scene with open lake and island, a seat of learning, a fortress, a history interwoven with old romance, linking us to great movements of a larger world. A town of three names, Indian, French and English, each recalling great days of our race, heroes of war and peace, men of insight and adventure, soldiers and statesmen—Frontenac, La Salle, Montcalm—and men of less note in the annals of the careless world, who perhaps did as much for mankind in laying the foundations of the British Empire, the "U.E." Loyalists, who settled Upper Canada, hacked it out of the forest, and then fought for it and kept it British.

§ 2. THE FRENCH KING AND HIS COLONISTS

"His Majesty's view", wrote the great Colbert on 17 May 1674, writing on behalf of his master, Louis XIV, "is not that you undertake great voyages by ascending the River St Lawrence, nor that the inhabitants spread themselves, for the future, farther than they have already done....He deems it more agreeable to the good of this service that you apply yourself to the clearing and settlement of those tracts which are most fertile and nearest the sea-coasts and the communication with France, than to think of distant discoveries in the interior of the country, so far off that they can never be settled or possessed by Frenchmen." Statesmen are so obviously sensible and wise; and there was wisdom and sense in this decision; by 1680, we are told, nine thousand French had landed in Canada, and had to the South of them English colonies settled fifty years before with twenty thousand immigrants, colonies daily increasing in numbers, wealth, and power. But a loophole was given by the Minister; Count Frontenac might take possession of countries "necessary to the trade and traffic of the French", if these were "open to discovery and occupation by any other nation that may disturb French commerce and trade"; and the nation to the South with its Indian allies had been all along and was to remain a great source of disturbance. Furthermore, Frontenac might establish himself in any country that offered France a sea communication from the interior more southerly than the St Lawrence. This gave the great Governor all he needed, and he had already anticipated the concession; our old city was the centre that was to safeguard trade and traffic against any other nation, and to open the door to a great river highway South of the St Lawrence.

"Quelques arpens de neige!" The quip of Voltaire is famous, but he is neither the first nor the last to find men of insight and imagination ridiculous. Founders of colonies and builders of empires have constantly met disaster, and only when they were gone has mankind reaped the fruit of their ideas. Eighty years after Frontenac planted his fort on Lake

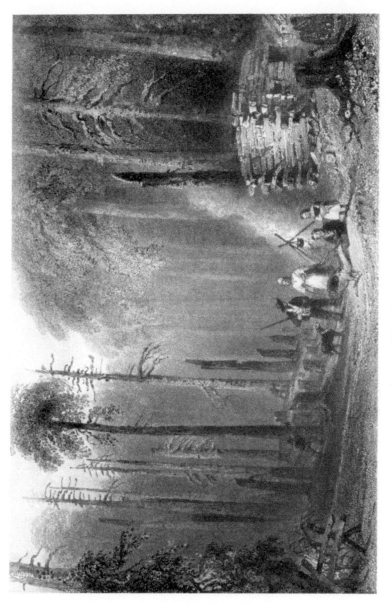

Plate I

A First Settlement

Ontario, England and France (Sir John Seeley reinforces Burke in this view) found in the fur trade one at least of the supreme causes for the Seven Years War. The fur trade was not among the reasons for the great Puritan emigration in 1628, perhaps not among the chief grounds for the occupation of Quebec by the French; but it soon became clear how significant the trade was. But the fur trade meant trapper and hunter, and the ranging of the forests and the lakes, ever farther and farther afield; the beaver would not, like the ducks in the nursery rhyme, "come and be killed". There was competition, fierce and keen, out in the wild; for peace was not the chief ambition of the Indian tribes; and the early settlers in Quebec in 1608 under Samuel Champlain had chosen the wrong side. They had allied themselves with the Hurons, and marched South with them to ravage the lands and villages of the Iroquois, who then realized for the first time the significance of fire-arms. The Iroquois were an intelligent race, already federated in their "Five Houses" by Hiawatha (or the historical fraction of Hiawatha), and they were quick to learn the lesson of this invasion. Fire-arms, and beaver-skins—and first the Dutch traders and later the English at the mouth of the Hudson; the Iroquois put two and two together, and the French for a century and a half had reason to lament Champlain's mistake, while the Hurons were practically harried out of existence.

The St Lawrence was the proper route for the fur trade, not the Hudson; but if the Iroquois were not controlled, if they were allowed to range to the North of what is now Lake Huron, and West of the Illinois where Chicago stands, Albany and New York would get the furs, not Montreal and Quebec. Frontenac's predecessor had seen this, and, with the gradual growth of knowledge of the Great Lakes, it became clearer that there must be some system of forts to keep the Iroquois out of these wider lands and to intercept the trade. Not everybody saw this; there was the argument for concentration, for strengthening and developing the colony already in being, which needed all the fostering it could have; the Roman clergy were divided—some troubled about the morals of the eager young men who broke away from farm and parish and became *coureurs de bois,* some apostolically eager for regions beyond; and there were commercial jealousies. Everybody who could contribute to the paralysing of enterprise found means to ply their arguments in Paris.

§ 3. LA SALLE AND LA CHINE

But when we look back, we find another series of ideas altogether. What had been the real intention of Columbus? Not to find America, North or South, but to sail to Cipangu, to Japan, to the Orient. Seventeen centuries before him a Greek geographer had maintained that the world was spherical, and therefore, if you could sail out of Spain and keep for ever to the same latitude (this is not a modern term), you would come to the Indies—only the world was so big and the ocean so great that you probably could never get across it; but, he was quite clear, if you *could* cross the Atlantic Sea, *there* was Eastern Asia. Eratosthenes had a very fairly true idea of the circumference of the earth; later on another and less accurate computation reduced the figure, and on this later estimate Columbus relied; the reduction had been taken out of the unsailed sea; he would not have to go as far as Eratosthenes had supposed. So he sailed, and he found, as we all know, lands which he, till he died, believed to be Asiatic; and the inhabitants are called Indians to this day.

But other men realized that the *Novus Orbis* was not the ancient Asia, and that, whatever charms the Spaniards might find in half-way houses as rich as Mexico and Peru, the real goal was beyond. They too were as eager for gold as the

Spaniards; but, failing lands of gold, which were continually promised and never reached, was there no strait that would take them to the East? Up the coast sailed Cabot, Verrazano, Hudson, Jacques Cartier, looking for a strait; down the coast sailed Amerigo, dotting the shore of Brazil with the names of the saints on whose days he touched; none of them, save Magellan to the very far South, found a strait, and a very awkward strait he found. If there were no straits, was there no other means of getting at the East? There was, as the great sonnet of Keats reminds us, even if he saw the wrong man "silent upon a peak in Darien". The Spaniards held the Isthmus of Panama, and, but for incursions of Francis Drake and his kind, they controlled the Pacific. They slowly made their way up the Pacific coast, past the dangerous Isle (no isle, but they thought so) to which was somehow attached the name borrowed from some old romance—California; some trade was established with China. Once a year a galleon went up past British Columbia to Alaska, crossed the narrow seas there, and coasted down Asia to China, traded and came back the same way. But it was not till the period of American independence—and then to anticipate English and Russian aggressions—that the Spanish settlements in Alta California were made—San Diego (1769), San Francisco (1776).

No strait but Magellan's, no isthmus but Panama; was there no other way? There were rumours, which gave hope. Behind the English colonies lay a great mountain range; somewhere, if you set out from the right colony, Virginia or Carolina, and climbed the range, you might get a glimpse Westward of another sea. Men said so; but no reliable European had yet seen it. But even if, just on the other side of the Cumberland gap, rolled the Pacific, that did not help the French. Nor were the English very sure of it, or they would not, in that sixteenth century and onward, have devoted so many men and ships to the quest of the North West passage, and the North East passage. True, the North East explorers found a way to Russia, an unexpected trade route; but beyond the White Sea they did not get far; and Russia was not the Orient.

Jacques Cartier in 1534 opened up for the French what might prove a more hopeful route—a route actually in use to-day, but not quite what was wanted then. The St Lawrence Gulf and River could be navigated to Montreal, and in 1608 Samuel Champlain made the small beginning of a great achievement; he planted his little colony of Quebec. In 1642 Maisonneuve founded Montreal on its island, below the inlet of the Ottawa and the impossible rapids, later on to bear the name Lachine. A hundred and sixty miles away was a huge freshwater lake, the name of which was to be decided. In a map of 1688 it is *Lac Frontenac, ou Ontario et Skaniadorio, ou St Louis*; and elsewhere the Lake of the Iroquois. Beyond this was another larger lake, inaccessible by water, cut off by a great cataract that might be spelled (and was spelled) *Onguiaahra*, or more simply *Ongiara*, which after about 1676 took its final form. To the North were other great lakes; but the goal lay Westward after all, and from the West came rumours of a Great Water. It must be the Pacific. The Creator, according to Champlain, had put the calculation of longitude beyond the power of man. The East coast of America was fairly mapped; the Spaniards knew something of the West coast, whatever they revealed of it; how far apart were the West and the East coasts? And till long afterwards geographers and seamen were haunted by the idea of a Strait of Anian. Suppose you carry your goods to a point beyond the rapids just above Montreal, you can sail to the far end of Lake St Louis or Ontario; there you will have to portage round Niagara, and Lake Erie is open to you; how far then will it be to the Great Water, and will there be no

rivers running into it? Find the river that runs into the Great
Water, and you have your route, all French, to China.
That was the dream of La Salle; and Colbert wrote that,
"after the increase of the colony, there is nothing more
important for that country and his Majesty's service than this
discovery of a passage to the South Sea". But the Mississippi
brought La Salle back by a long, weary, and difficult way to
the Atlantic. The only China he ever found was his farm by
the side of the rapids; La Chine his mocking neighbours called
it, and Lachine it remains. The taunt keeps the memory of
a great story and of a great man; and however he felt about
it himself, a later day counts it all to his honour.

La Salle found no route to China, but he learnt how easy
it was to link the St Lawrence with the Mississippi. It had
not been easy for him; but he had shown how France might
forestall "discovery and occupation by any other nation that
may disturb French commerce and trade". A fort where the
St Lawrence leaves Lake Ontario; a fort at Niagara; a colony
at or near the mouth of the Mississippi; these for a beginning,
easily to be made, and the gap gradually to be filled. New
Orleans in name, in tradition, and to some extent in speech,
is French to this day, a colony from Canada planted by one
of the great house of Le Moyne. But the key position was
obviously a fortress on the Ontario strand where Kingston
stands. Whether you think of the control of the Iroquois, of
the route to China, or the checking of English expansion, a
fort on Lake Ontario was the first step, every way necessary.
And two great men achieved it.

§ 4. THE FOUNDING OF FORT FRONTENAC

In 1672 Count Frontenac came out to govern the little colony
of Canada, with its French population of something under
7000 persons, and this in spite of much fostering and the
thoughtful export of brides. No wonder that French historians

of that century hardly mention the country. No wonder that wise statesmen were against scattering so small a population over a huge continent.

Frontenac had come to Canada, by all accounts, a ruined man of fifty-two. Marriage and property had gone wrong; and, as with so many, there was nothing for him but the colonies. He also had the gift of incurring enmity, by luck or by management. But, with all his limitations, he was a man, and he knew a man when he saw him, and saw with the eyes of a soldier and an empire-builder. His predecessor had seen that it was desirable to have a French fort where the St Lawrence leaves Lake Ontario; Frontenac built it. And when a weak successor destroyed it, Frontenac on his return to Canada, the only French governor twice sent out, rebuilt it.

On 3 June 1673 he set out from Quebec, and taking a look at various posts along the river, he reached Montreal on 15 June. On the 30th, with a force of some 400, French and Indian, in 120 canoes and two flat-boats, he set out to navigate the river. The rapids involved prodigious labour, in which Frontenac himself took a hand. The expedition was to succeed. He writes to France of "the most beautiful piece of country that can be imagined", the river strewn with islands, forest-clad with oak and other hardwoods—the river banks no less charming with forest and meadow and wild flowers; it might be improved by some clearing, he added. The beauty of the river is famous in spite of clearing.

On 12 July they reached the head of the river, and rounding Cedar Island saw the site that was to be historic. There was an alternative; might not some point up on the Bay of Quinte serve better? But no! Here the Cataraqui fell into the Lake, and the St Lawrence left it, and here should be the fort. The historians of the old city love to linger over the scene, the summer day, the great flotilla, the Count (an artist in the use of pomp), and the gathering of Indians, and—while "pre-

Plate II

Fort Henry

liminary civilities" were being exchanged—the rapid felling
of timber and the quick erection of a defensible fort. And
the address of the Count!—his words on religion with its
double duty of love to God and love to man—a conception
of life not fully realized by the Iroquois for some generations
(at this point he gave them fifteen guns, with powder, lead
and flints)—and other words, more intelligible, about trade,
"all sorts of refreshments and commodities, which I shall
cause to be furnished to you at the cheapest rate possible",
though, as he hinted, the cost of transport was high. At this
point twenty-five large overcoats were distributed. He wished
peace among the tribes—Iroquois, Algonquins and all; he
would like to educate some of their children. One or two
shrewd questions were asked; the Iroquois, indeed the Indian
generally, seems all along to have had business instincts.
And by 20 July Fort Frontenac was completed, and a few
days later, leaving behind him a good understanding well
established and good hopes for the future, Frontenac went
down the river. The fort had cost 10,000 francs. A year later
came a scolding from Paris; consolidation was the word,
not expansion, not "great voyages ascending the river St
Lawrence". But he was able to reply that his fortress had
produced the best results—more Indians than ever coming
to Montreal—peace among the tribes—the Jesuits reporting
their position improved; still, if the Minister disapproves,
Frontenac will go up the river again and destroy the fort.
But it did not yet come to that.

La Salle now comes into our story, and to a far greater
extent than most of us remember at Kingston. In 1674 he
visited Paris, and asked for a patent of nobility in recognition
of his work as an explorer, and for a grant in seigniory of
Fort Frontenac. He would repay the King the 10,000 francs,
maintain a garrison, by and by build a church, and settle
domesticated Indians in the neighbourhood. Both his peti-

tions were granted. Within two years he replaced the wooden fort with a stone one, much larger, with ramparts and bastions. He cleared a hundred French acres, planted them in part, fetched cattle, fowls and swine from Montreal; and built four ships for service on lake and river; and, wrote a friend, "if he had preferred gain to glory, he had only to stay at his fort". But he was of another type, as history knows—the most splendid type, perhaps the greatest figure, in the story of French Canada. To his travels, his troubles and triumphs, we must not digress; but it is part of the great legend of the town of three names that this man ruled here and made Fort Frontenac his base for his great work of opening up America; and that Frontenac repeatedly visited the place.

But in 1682 Frontenac was superseded as Governor by Lefebvre de la Barre, while a man called Meulles became Intendant. Their quality may be judged by two sentences. Meulles opined that "it is of very great importance that the people should not be allowed to speak their minds"; while La Barre received a letter from the King, saying, "I am persuaded with you that Sieur de la Salle's discovery [of the mouth of the Mississippi] is very useless, and such enterprises must be prevented hereafter". La Barre seized Fort Frontenac, or his agents did, and wasted La Salle's goods and lands. La Salle went straight to France, and the King vindicated him, and ordered reparation (1684).

Worse was to follow. La Barre was succeeded by Denonville, who floundered into war with the Iroquois. He treacherously seized a number of Onondagas who had come obviously peaceably, for they brought wives and children, to Fort Frontenac, and he packed off the men, some thirty-five, to France to be made galley slaves. Before they left, the Mission Indians tortured them. The Iroquois rejoined with a proper massacre of French at Lachine and a murdering rampage over the Island of Montreal. Denonville was in

Montreal and thought the defensive was best. Dongan, the Governor of New York, joined with the Iroquois in demanding the destruction of Fort Frontenac, and at the end of his tether and his tenure Denonville consented. He sent orders to the garrison to blow up the walls, destroy the stores and fall back on Montreal. And it was done, before the countermanding orders of Frontenac could arrive.

For Frontenac was returning to Canada. He sailed from France on the actual day of the Lachine massacre (5 August 1689). Of the rest of his acts we have not to speak, but at last the fort that bore his name was restored in 1695; once again French intrigue came near thwarting him; but it failed. The mining of the walls had been hastily done, and the damage to them was far less than the damage to French prestige had been. An expeditionary force of 700, at a cost this time of 16,000 francs, put the fort in a condition of defence in a month, and left a garrison of forty-eight. After which the King suggested further consultations as to whether a fort at that spot was really desirable. Frontenac thought it was. He died at Quebec, 28 November 1698. La Salle had died eleven years earlier.

For fifty years their fortress stood, a vital link in the chain of forts on which French ambitions depended. We read how, a quarter of a century after Frontenac, the English built Oswego in what is now New York State to offset it, and how, thus challenged, the French built vessels of war at Frontenac and started a secondary fort 174 miles away, which they called Toronto, to intercept the northern fur trade and keep it out of English hands.

When the last great war broke out between English and French in Canada, Fort Frontenac was one of the crucial positions. "If", writes Captain John Shirley in 1755 to the Governor of Pennsylvania, "we take or destroy their two vessels at Frontenac and ruin their harbour there, and

destroy the two forts of that and Niagara, I shall think we
have done great things." Both places were strongly held.
By now there was no doubt among the French as to the
value of Count Frontenac's ideas. But in 1755 Shirley's plans
miscarried; troops at Fort Frontenac frustrated him; and it
was the year of Braddock's destruction by the Indians. Next
year the great Montcalm himself was at Fort Frontenac, and
from there crossed the lake to capture Oswego—"the greatest
triumph that French arms had yet achieved in America",
says Parkman; France was mistress of the lake, mistress of
the ways to the West; Shirley had not cut French Canada in
two; and the possession of Fort Frontenac had been decisive.

Three years later the fortunes of war turned the other way.
In August 1758 Bradstreet, with 3000 men and a fleet of whale-
boats and bateaux, sailed out on the lake, and three days later
landed near Fort Frontenac. They were an overwhelming
force. On 27 August the French commander surrendered
himself, his 110 soldiers, the fort, sixty cannon, the fleet of
nine armed vessels, munitions, and Indian goods for the
western trade. The crews of the French fleet escaped somehow. The French guns were used for battering down the
French walls; the fort was dismantled, everything that could
be burned, buildings or ships (two excepted to carry booty),
was burned. The French no longer could command the lake;
New France was cut in two decisively; next to the fall of
Louisbourg it was the heaviest blow that France had yet
had—a prelude to the fall of Quebec next year. "This is a
glorious piece of news, and may God have all the glory of the
same", writes an English chaplain.

For a quarter of a century the place lay in ruins. One
power held the continent North of the Spanish territory;
there was no need to fight for the control of the great West;
there was no one to contest possession of the lake. The old
chain of French forts was broken, all that mattered were in

English hands. Trade went its own way. The place that had been the key to all was now of no immediate interest; but when the continent was again divided, the old story began over again, with keener passions.

So ends the French period of our city; and when one reflects on the three great names Frontenac, La Salle, and Montcalm, all significant, meeting here where the river leaves the lake; when one thinks of all the issues bound up with their ambitions, their achievements and their failures, issues ranging from Paris to China, great adventures, discoveries, tragedies, and all finding a centre in that quiet little corner of Canada (so far it seems to-day from being the centre of anything), one can understand how, to those who love the past, and for whom the past lives, the little town has an appeal of its own. So great is the story—*et quorum pars magna fui*, the town might say, if it could take voice and quote Virgil—*our* town, we say; and the reader can guess what we are thinking. But that is not all the story.

§ 5. THE UNITED EMPIRE LOYALISTS

In 1776 the "Declaration of Independence" was signed. To-day the folly of English politicians, whose theories and prejudices gave the excuse for rebellion, has been abundantly recognized. Long ago Britain abandoned conspicuously any attempt to do again what Parliament tried to do in the bad years that led to the outbreak. Whether America has ceased to be proud of the extremists who led her to independence is another matter, and does not concern us. The Tories, as those were labelled who did not want revolution—the Loyalists—have their story to tell of those years, a story which English people at large have forgotten, much as the Empire owes to those men, for few have done so much to make it. It is intelligible that Americans do not generally care to remind their neighbours or posterity of what was done.

"C. H. Van Tyne's *Loyalists in the American Revolution* is the standard work", wrote Edward Channing of Harvard; they were both Americans, and historians of high standing; and what follows comes largely from Van Tyne and not from British sources.

Side by side with the courtesy that all visitors recognize there runs a marked vein of brutality through American life, the despair of the better elements, always rather powerless in a democracy of the extreme type. To-day it is polite to associate this with that stream of undesirable immigrants, which for two generations after 1850 flowed in ever-increasing volume into the States from eastern and southern Europe, and from Ireland. But to the reader of American history it is evident that America had little to learn from the undesirables: the bad streak is a legacy from old frontier days when Indian scalped white man, and white man scalped Indian, and law was not, when the aphorism ruled that the only good Indian was a dead Indian. When the negro is lynched—or tried at Scottsborough—it is not so much evidence as hatred or hysteria that dictates the proceedings; and law yields place to mere antipathy. Once let American feeling, or fear, be roused, and you are back on the frontier, Kentucky or Wyoming; and there is little safety in law for the victim, or in anything else.

So the Loyalists found. Mobs and the destruction of property, and tarring and feathering, came first—the "Sons of Liberty"; by and by Committees took charge of these duties. Loyalists were harried by rebel militia; they were disarmed and disfranchised, fined for exercising their professions, jailed in Philadelphia, city of saints; they had to make good stolen property, whoever stole it; their goods were raffled by the authorities, confiscation being recommended by a resolution of Congress in 1777; and these amenities did not stop when peace was made. Mr Van Tyne gives a classified catalogue of legislation passed against them by one state and another—laws forbidding freedom of speech, and dealing with the crime of adhering to Britain. But all this was not the work of mobs and Sam Adamses—the "virtuous", as all upholders of independence were now labelled. The British people have decided that Washington was an honourable adversary. It is significant, then, that Washington was outspoken in his detestation of our fellow-citizens—they were "abominable pests of society" against whom vigorous measures ought to be taken. He suggested to the Governor of Rhode Island the expediency of seizing those "we know will be against us...whilst we know that they will do us every mischief in their power". (This is surely Looking-Glass way, punishment first, verdict after, and crime last.) He talked at large of their "diabolical and insidious arts". These vicious people constituted very largely the educated and professional element in their communities, as General Washington very well knew. He even suggested that suicide was their proper course. But we need not vituperate Washington; that has been done, adequately, by the rival patriot, Thomas Jefferson, author of the Declaration and of nearly everything unsound in American life.

In 1783 the American rebellion ended in victory. American arms, the genius of Washington, the French fleet and Lafayette, the neglect of the British navy, and English divisions, ended a war in which Britain had been half-hearted from the first. If Dr Johnson roared his indignation at the rebels, Boswell stood up for them. The Great Lakes were once more to be the boundary between rival nations, each more and more alive to the value of the West and the North West. Flushed with triumph the Republicans turned upon the defeated Loyalists, in spite of safeguards and conditions embodied in the treaty. Great Britain was to learn then, as other nations have had to learn since, how difficult is the position when one central or Federal Government makes a treaty, and leaves it—in this case "recommended" it—to thirteen independent if federated states to carry out as they may choose. The American constitution seems designed to frustrate negotiation with any other nation.

There was naturally a rush of Loyalists for safety to British territory. Many went to Britain, among them Flora Macdonald, once friend in need to Prince Charles Edward, with her husband, while their son went to Canada. Twenty-five thousand sought Canada at once, some thirty-five thousand the Maritimes, though of these many moved on during the following spring to Ontario. A new town grew up around the ruins of Count Frontenac's famous fort, and the place received its third name. It is not difficult to guess why it was called Kingston—with Queenston at the upper end of the lake, and names borrowed from the Royal House here and there on the shore between, notably York, once Fort Toronto, but now named after the Royal Duke, who was to remodel the English army and give Wellington the tool he needed. Kingston became the first centre, whence settlement spread into five townships westward along the lake and eight down the river.

The journey to freedom had been terrible for many of the refugees who came by land; and preferable as the forest to which they came might be to the republic which they were glad to leave, many of them had not been used to forest conditions; and Ontario was still covered with primeval forest. The working-class people fell more easily into the new life than those more used to refinement. Life was hard enough for all; and the winters were long and Canadian. There was plenty of firewood to be had for the felling; but for three or four years food had to come by water from Montreal, and 160 miles was a long journey while roads were yet to make, and long enough when they were made.

1788 was long remembered as "the hungry year"; crops had failed in 1787, and the sheep designed to clothe the community were eaten by their owners, sharing them reluctantly with bears and wolves. Ere long (1793) a bounty of $4 a head had to be given for the destruction of wolves. The Mohawk Indians, settled not far away—for they too had to leave the States with their allies—understood the forest better and helped the white settlers, particularly in hunting the deer. But 1789 made amends with a good season. In time, hard work and courage made a new country and a pleasant one; and it does not hurt a nation to have great memories, and to be conscious that it was founded on principle and built up by heroism. The danger comes when the fathers are forgotten, and their sufferings and their principles become unintelligible.

But America was not done with the Loyalists. Not quite thirty years had they been in their new homes when "Mr Madison's War" threatened to undo all. Napoleon was fighting England, and England was interfering with American shipping. So was Napoleon, who seized 150 ships in one year. England was searching American ships to find her own deserting seamen aboard them. But "the American Government was, to say the least, not unwilling to be deceived" by the Emperor, if Britain could be injured and Mr Madison re-elected. It was supposed that Canada would be an easy prey. Jefferson, Monroe, Calhoun are all on record as of this belief; it would be "a mere matter of marching"—"in four weeks from the time a declaration of war is heard on our frontier, the whole of Upper Canada and a part of Lower Canada will be in our power". Britain had all she could do to fight Napoleon; and there had been already an American emigration to Canada, and on these immigrants the Americans could surely rely. America in men and resources was far the stronger on the continent. It was forgotten—or neglected—

that the Loyalists were not American in sentiment; that they remembered things that happened thirty years before. They were assured indeed that they would be "emancipated from tyranny and oppression, and restored to the dignified station of freemen". America has always believed in the potency of a rolling period. There was no telegraph, and it was not known that Napoleon was in retreat from Moscow; or perhaps there might have been no war.

But war there was; and a chain of places were recognized to be significant—Mackinac and Detroit westward, and nearer the sea Kingston and Montreal. To capture either Kingston or Montreal would cut that connection with the sea which was vital to British Canada. Kingston was the largest and most populous settlement in Upper Canada; and its capture, says Admiral Mahan, "would solve at a single stroke every difficulty in the upper territory. No other harbour was tenable as a naval station; with its fall and the destruction of shipping and forts would go the control of the lake, even if the place itself were not permanently held." It was, says Professor Channing, "the strategic point of attack, second only to Montreal". For Britain too recognized the significance of the place, and massed there such troops as she could and built ships of war. Navy Bay was full of ship-building; "120 ship-carpenters have arrived, and more are expected", announced the Kingston *Gazette*, while 400 or 500 seamen from the Royal Navy—"as fine-looking fellows as ever were beheld!"—were landed at Halifax and sent overland to the lake. In 1813 two thousand troops under Major-General Rottenburg garrisoned the town. But with war to the East and war to the West, Kingston, the centre of British operations, was not itself attacked—though it was always marked down for attack and destruction. York, Newark and Brockville were burned, public buildings and private, by the Americans, who have never ceased to be shocked that Washington, so far as public buildings went, should suffer the same fate by way of reprisal.

It is not our task here to write the history of Mr Madison's war; Kingston is our theme—Kingston, vital to Empire and Republic, threatened, garrisoned, and unassailed; and there for us the story of the war is told. Napoleon fell, and Mr Madison made peace in 1815—a lucky peace, in which he got off better than he deserved, for his negotiators served him more ably than his soldiers; and—to the lasting loss of Canada—no frontier was rectified; so generous or absent-minded are British diplomats. But Canada gained some things by the war. The sense of nationality was developing; the stream of immigrants from the States was stopped, and Americanization halted; and a new immigration from Scotland and England began in earnest.

The war was over—but not in four weeks. And a message came from the Prince Regent in "words, as graceful as they were true", says the historian. "Nor is His Royal Highness insensible to the merits of the inhabitants of Upper Canada, or to the great assistance which the militia of the province afforded during the whole of the war. His Royal Highness trusts that you will express to them in adequate terms the high sense which he entertains of their services as having mainly contributed to the immediate preservation of the province and its future security."

§ 6. AFTER MR MADISON'S WAR

This was the last that the old town saw of actual war. But the threat has constantly been repeated. If President Polk and the American Senate in 1846 accepted latitude 49° as the international boundary from Lake Superior to the Pacific, the great "slogan" of his election campaign in 1844 had been "fifty-four forty or fight"; and steps were taken to strengthen the defences of Kingston and to have vessels built on the lake that could be used as gunboats. But Polk confined himself to expansion at the cost of Mexico. Again in 1861 when Captain Wilkes of the U.S. Navy took Mason and Slidell off a British ship, the *Trent*, it was long before Lincoln and his cabinet, with their eyes on their supporters, surrendered the two men, but without an apology. Neither government had really wanted war, but it had come so very near that British reinforcements had been despatched to Canada. After the American Civil War, Seward in 1869 urged the "cession" of Canada to balance the *Alabama* claims, but these were referred to Geneva and assessed at fifteen and a half million dollars, which the sufferers from the depredations of that ship never drew in full. In 1866 various Fenian groups had threatened or invaded Canada; and there must still have been those who remembered Sam Houston and his doings in Texas, and took "filibustering" as a prelude to something more. The Fenians after defeat on Canadian soil were arrested in New York State and promptly released; and no claims of the *Alabama* kind were made, or honoured by the government which had failed to maintain neutrality; elections had been imminent, Professor S. E. Morison notices. Later again, in December 1895, eleven months before a presidential election, President Cleveland in the affair of Venezuela threatened Britain with war; but after "a frenzy of jingoism throughout the United States", followed by a fall in stocks, both nations rallied to the view of the aged Gladstone—"Only common sense is needed". In 1903 Theodore Roosevelt informed the British Government that, if the agreed tribunal awarded the Alaskan shore to Canada, he would not respect the award; he believed (in his own phrase) in "speaking softly and carrying a big stick", a form of negotiation not always acceptable in Europe; but Sir Richard Webster secured that Roosevelt was satisfied.

This list of threatening moments is incomplete and can remain so.

In review of all these threats and menaces it ceases to be strange to find what steps Britain took to secure Kingston. Blockhouses were built round the town in 1812; new barracks in 1824; Fort Henry between 1832 and 1836; the Martello towers in 1846, President Polk's time; and above all the Rideau canal system was made at the cost of a million sterling or more to the Old Country tax-payer. This project, very dear to the great Duke of Wellington, was to give us another waterway from Montreal to the Upper Lakes, which should not, like the St Lawrence, during a part of its flow, be commanded from an American shore. *Si vis pacem, para bellum,* says the old adage, and in spite of modern theorists (and Jefferson was one of them) it has still a certain wisdom.

But war did not come again. In the harbour, in the park, over at Fort Henry and Fort Frederick, and on Cedar Island, stand the beautiful Martello towers—monuments now rather than defences; and, when Kingston wakes up to a sense of its own beauty and its history, it will make the Federal Government restore them. And who would wish to be without the pleasant Rideau canal, even if its construction was a military measure, and if its utility in case of war might to-day perhaps be slight?

Times have changed. The West and the North West are full of people. The explorer has yielded place to the farmer and the prospector. Fifty years have seen the great cities grow from Winnipeg to Vancouver. Kingston is no longer an outlying fort. In the old days of which we have been thinking, the river was the one way from Montreal to the West; beyond were the lakes and Indian trails. The railways have changed all that, and to them has been added the immense network of modern roads. If war comes again, it is probable that it will bring out new plans of campaign; but Kingston will still be a frontier town. But, not to plan horror and tragedy that we would all avoid, we can look back with pride to a great past, and we can enjoy an old town in a great setting, the Great Lake, the matchless river, and islands near and far, at sunset and at dawn, in clear weather and in storm, ice-bound or with open water, always beautiful.

Chapter II

THE TOWN WE KNEW

§ I. RAIL AND RIVER

There were two ways from Montreal to Kingston when we were young. You could go by rail or you could go by steamer. No doubt there was a road; there had been in fact for two generations or more; but once the Grand Trunk Railway was opened in 1856 from Montreal to Toronto, who went by road? Perhaps not even the tramps; they too preferred the rail, if they only stole rides on freight-cars. In our youth the train took some six hours to reach Kingston, about half the time spent on the 333 miles to Toronto, which, long as it was, was two hours quicker than in 1856. It is not without emotion that after forty years one comes to the Bonaventure station in Montreal and finds it practically unchanged. Similarly at the Kingston outer station not a brick seems replaced, not an inch of woodwork retouched with paint—

> So was it when my life began;
> So is it now I am a man;
> And I could wish—

Esto perpetua! Let Kingston keep some at least of her antiquities!

It was a long ride, with halts at many stations and hardly a name familiar to the newcomer from the old land. Cornwall, of course, is on English maps, but it has not a railway station, it is not a riverside town. Brockville says nothing until you know the story of the gallant Isaac Brock and his victory at Queenston Heights in the War of 1812. Gananoque was another new name; of course we give *qu* its English value and perhaps we are right—did not the French once spell our town

Cataracoui? Certainly the American was wrong who made Gananoque into three French syllables to rhyme with *équivoque*; you can be too peregrinate. Between these places and Kingston there is a new interest in the countryside. All the way, in those old years of the 'nineties, the newcomer was struck with one thing, odd in a new country; how bare it was of trees, compared with the country you see from the English Great Western! Settler and farmer had done their work only too well. As Thomas Paddock wrote home from near Galt (21 June 1835) about an old acquaintance: "The most suitable man for this country would be Tom Price; no one would send him (to) gaol for stealing timber but would thank him for taking it". But time has done something to heal the injury. The forests are not replaced; but there is a beauty returning to the landscape; trees, that will not make timber, will grow if you let them alone, and others may spring up beside them; Nature is sometimes kinder than man.

Unchanged, however, are the great rocks. Others must explain the "Laurentian shield" that seems to a layman to stretch from Connecticut to the far end of Lake Superior, and makes a country rich in innumerable lakes which man cannot abolish as he did the forests—a country as different as you can conceive from the 800 miles of prairie that separate it from the Rockies, which are different again. Here along our G.T.R. great shoulders and boulders of granite stand out among the cow pastures—round and smooth as skulls, ground to that shape, the learned tell us, by glaciers long ago, gaunt reminders of a remote geological past. The forest that a hundred years ago flourished about them is gone; and the white man's Holstein cow stands in the sun chewing the cud on the bare round top, the mullein towering its three feet where the pine once towered its ninety, and the golden rod flaming in the zigzags of the old snake fence along which the chipmunk runs. Next comes the cornfield with what the

English will call Indian corn, with more unconscious gratitude than you would expect. Read *Hiawatha* if you want to know how beautiful it is. The field stays in memory from that first vision of it on the late September day, the splendid corn on the little hillocks, and lolling on the ground beneath in gorgeous orange the huge pumpkins—green and orange—and the cloudless blue sky over all. Don't tell us that there is no beauty in the Canadian landscape, even in these poor townships. Read the countryside sonnets of Charles G. D. Roberts, and you may understand how we feel about the clearing and the creek where the cattle come to drink. He may be a Nova Scotian, but he makes one homesick for a small bay of Lake Ontario.

But if you have time on your hands and will not fret at delay in the six canals which must take the up-bound steamer past Lachine and the other rapids, you can come up by river. Leisurely travel, it took some thirty hours, but it is something to know the great river from the lake to the sea. In another chapter something will be said of the trip *down* the river at the level of the water. Even on the steamer it is worth while; the first time you may crowd with the others to the bow to see the rapids you shoot and the terrible table-edge rocks; the next time you will watch the pilot and the man at the wheel, and wonder perhaps which is the more impressive sight. But come *up* the river if you would see what Frontenac saw in 1673, what the Loyalists saw in 1784 after their winter at Sorel. You will read of Frontenac's memorable expedition in the stately pages of Francis Parkman—why doesn't England know him better? Centuries have passed since Frontenac rounded headland and island and saw the place for his fortress, but you can still voyage with him. Man has done his worst on the place—shaved smooth the hill where Fort Henry stands, made Wolfe Island a farm country, and set on the main shore a town with church towers, hideous elevators and an appalling bridge—and yet has not been able to spoil that marvellous scene. The town is half lost in its maples; you forget the shaven hill; lake and river defy the spoiling hand of man and speak to you of history, of Nature and of God. The breadth of the expanse, the stillness, the very wonder (is it childish?) that there is so much fresh water in the world, speak "rememberable things". Our waters—the land of Frontenac, the land of the Loyalists, full of their memories and traditions—and we see what they saw.

Once I lay for five weeks in the Kingston General Hospital, with the lake for company. Here at Kingston it is not as at Toronto, with an island shutting off the lake from you, nor as at Chicago where you look out over unbroken waters to the horizon. Here there are nearer islands, and islands further away, great islands and small, and in among them is a great opening where the lake reaches out to the sky. It was over this stretch of it that I looked for those weeks, and in the middle of it was Snake Island with its little clump of trees some four miles away. My room was high up; I saw nothing of the town or the land but a few tree tops; all the view was lake. Day by day I watched for Snake Island in the dawn; day by day I watched it grow dim in the dusk; and the hours between—how can I speak of all I saw?—sunrise and sunset and moonlight—the sea of glass shining like that the Apostle saw from Patmos (have I not seen that too, and do not both bring you near heaven?)—and then the storm raging down the two hundred miles from Niagara. Do you wonder that the hospital has pleasant memories quite apart from the kindness of nurses and old friends? Yes, the lake is good company: and when all was dark the lake steamers would come and call for pilots. Past and present, great history and eternal beauty—and some Old World people think our New World dull. We know better.

Plate III

The St Lawrence from Fort Henry

§ 2. THE FAMOUS NAMES

History is written all over our town, and the history is not
lost in the savourless expansion that makes some cities so
proud of their wilderness of new streets and "beautiful
homes", without architecture or character, in long rows, that
might be anywhere else from Cape Cod to Seattle. We have
historians, too. Agnes Maule Machar printed a history of
Kingston some thirty years ago; but the men she consulted
were shy of her efforts—one of them protesting that he did
not choose to belong to the generation before his father. But
the impetuous lady cared for none of these things. "Agnes,"
said a woman friend, "you did well for that honeymoon
couple in your last novel—giving them a full moon for six
weeks." "Yes, I know," rejoined the novelist, "but I knew
no one would notice it but you." Of course there are different
views of history; and if you love Kingston and have somebody
to rearrange the dates (or perhaps share her superiority to
such trifles), you will find much of interest in Miss Machar's
book. Typescript collections made with more care by Mr
Edwin Horsey and (especially about the hospital) by Mr Hugh
C. Nickle will give you—or if only they reach the print they
deserve, they will give you—endless detail. Every corner has
its story, *nullum sine nomine saxum*, for a century and a half;
and the names are not names of nobodies but of men who
built in a corner but built for an empire. It makes one think
of Zion in the old Psalm:

> Thy saints take pleasure in her stones,
> Her very dust to them is dear.

Kingston—the name has history in it, as we have seen, and
the islands round about speak of the past—Wolfe, Amherst
and Simcoe. Simcoe was Governor from 1792 to 1799, the
friend of Wilberforce, and he struck the same note as to

slavery from his first coming. "The moment I assume the government of Upper Canada, under no modification will I assent to a law that discriminates by dishonest policy between the natives of Africa, America or Europe." On another page will be found a hint of what the negro has owed to Canada. The streets tell of our past. King Street and Queen Street in all our towns come naturally; the Loyalists meant something by the names; every mention of the streets spoke of resolve and sacrifice—yes, and to later days they may speak of achievement. Princess Street had been prosaically Store Street, but when Queen Victoria's first child was born, in 1842, the name was changed; and, as the town expanded westward, place was found for the Princess's father, and sister, and the Duke of Edinburgh, in Albert, Alice and Alfred Streets. Bagot, Brock, Colborne and Sydenham in the older part speak of men who moulded the Dominion. Wellington, next above King, suggests date and history; and no one can grudge Count Frontenac a street in his own town. But less familiar names have their place too. Johnson Street does not always remind everybody of the great Indian agent, Sir William Johnson, friend of the loyal Mohawk, Joseph Brant (whom George Romney painted) and husband of the famous Molly Brant; but he had his part in our story and he deserves remembrance. The quaintest set of names recalls a churchly family of old days. John Stuart, the earliest Church of England parson of the town, left a son and successor in Archdeacon George Okill Stuart, in whose house, long the centre of Queen's College, lives the Principal; and when roads were made on his great property, once called Stuartsville, he distributed his names and titles over them, and Arch, Deacon, George, Okill and Stuart are the streets about the University to this day; an innocent piece of ingenuity.

But before we drift into the town, there is something to be said for following up our previous study and realizing something of nineteenth-century Canada and its work and problems. Here to the North of the town, very much on the site of the old Fort Frontenac, stand the British Tête du Pont barracks. In the yard there used to be shown an outline of stones that marked the foundations of the French fort. Here from the early days of the Loyalists were in turn Royal Scots and many other regiments from the Old Country, till Canada undertook to supply her own garrisons. In the 'forties it cost the British tax-payer half a million sterling a year to safeguard Canada. Nor was that all, for the great Rideau canal system, which issues hard by the barracks, through the Cataraqui river into the lake, cost more than a million. The Rideau lakes are beautiful and suggest little beyond peace and rest; but they, with the Rideau river falling into the Ottawa and this Cataraqui, were linked up over the height of land with forty-six locks, to make a waterway for men and munitions to the great navy centre on the lake—a waterway that should not skirt the American shore. The imperial authorities brooded over the scheme for thirty-six years, and at last, when Mr Madison's War was ten years behind them, they began the work in 1826 and completed it in 1832. There was a pleasant old legend that the American Government in making peace in 1815 agreed to pay Britain a million pounds, and that the Duke of Wellington got it spent on the canal. There have been remarkable expenditures by American governments to acquire territory from Napoleon, Santa Anna the Mexican president, and the Czar; but this payment seems alas! mythical.

Beyond the Cataraqui lies Fort Frederick with the Royal Military College, Navy Bay, famous during the War of 1812 and after, and Fort Henry on the headland between the rivers. Fort Henry does not bear a royal name; like the most famous spot in North America, the Plains of Abraham, it commemorates a man otherwise forgotten. Abraham Martin, a French pilot, owned those plains above Quebec; Henry Hamilton was Lieutenant-Governor, 1782–5; and from Point Henry Fort Henry took its name. A log fort in 1812, a stone one in 1820, preceded the present fort, about which legend has much to tell us; the Duke of Wellington designed the plan, but some clerk sent to Kingston, Jamaica, the plan meant for us and theirs to Kingston, Canada; or it was "built the wrong way round", and that is why a second fort was added, opening out of the first; and so forth. But the Duke's plans were never in the local paper, and experts are less sure than amateurs that the whole thing was a heap of blunders; but here, as elsewhere, the amateurs do most of the talking. Kingston, as history had shown, was assailable by lake and by land; the navy could be relied on to do its part on the water; Martello towers should guard the harbour; and the fort, the first in a chain of six, was to do its share in case of attack on the landward side; and to protect docks and canal. The other five were never built; in spite of many threats and occasional semi-private raids, the United States seemed unlikely to make war, and, hoping for the best, the British House of Commons refused to go further with the scheme. The fort dates from 1836, the Martello towers were built ten years later. For forty years now fort and towers have been left to the care of the climate. Perhaps some parts of it were put in order in 1914 when 200 Austrian reservists were interned there. They had tried to travel through southern Ontario on their way from Chicago to New York to sail for Europe, but were invited to leave the train after it had passed under the Detroit river. The wooden roofs of the beautiful Martello towers have rotted or been blown off; frost has done its work on the pointing of the well-built walls; and the Kingston limestone, in spite of local pride, is of poor quality, splitting and cracking in the most lamentable way. At last, and none too soon, the Dominion Government has roused itself to

Plate IV

Kingston from Fort Henry

repair the fort, and some day perhaps it will think of the towers. The old block houses are all torn down, the last only a few years ago despite the efforts of General Ross, M.P. for the city, to save it from Vandal hands. Things are sometimes done better in the States; and a visit to the fort at Ticonderoga, restored and refitted with old period guns, proudly bearing G *III* and L *XV* upon them—gifts from the British and French governments—might teach some of our rulers that antiquity has, apart from spiritual considerations, even a financial value. Kingston has a story and has monuments beyond any city above Montreal; Toronto conspicuously has neither; and one might expect a certain pride in those we elect to rule us. But on neither side of the line, or of the ocean, has imagination ever been the distinguishing mark of a town council. Imagination is a delicate plant, scarcely to be grafted.

The town on one side of the Cataraqui outlet, Navy Bay and the fort on the other, with prospects of the greater fort to be built—it was clear that people would not always be content with ferries. At last a company was formed in 1827 to build a bridge, an Act obtained to empower it to do so, £6000 raised, and in due time the old wooden bridge we knew spanned the Cataraqui—1800 feet long, 25 feet wide, and resting on stone piers 40 feet apart to permit the passage of cribs of timber, with a special swing bridge to let shipping through, a width of 18 feet being thought enough for this. Tolls were levied to recoup the promoters—7½*d*. for a two-horse vehicle; 6*d*., if you drove only one horse; 5*d*., if you rode your horse; 1*d*., if you went on foot; and the last charge gave the bridge its name, the "Penny Bridge"—not that it needed a name, for there was no other bridge near the town. Foot-passengers, if recollection serves, no longer paid pennies in our day; but the memory is vivid of the structure of planks, ageing as they lay, creaking and even rattling as you went across, a horror to bicyclists, a picturesque old-time affair, doomed as soon as there were motorists to insist on a surface fit for their wheels. The first motor car appeared in Kingston in the winter of 1900–1; it was Dr Black's. The Kingston horses disliked it so much that he gave up driving it. Yet by 1916 the old bridge was gone and its place taken by a terribly efficient "Causeway", honoured with the name of La Salle, and more hideous than anything he ever saw or dreamed of in his seigniory. It was the work of the Canadian Government. It is indeed curious how uniformly the official mind reflects: "Here is a place of exceptional beauty, let us put a grain-elevator, a prison, a madhouse in it, at any rate *something* dispiriting." Such is the story of our town.

One government creation, however, is happier. When Lord Dufferin was Governor-General and Alexander Mackenzie Premier (who in his mason days had worked in the building of Fort Henry), the Royal Military College came into being. It stands in the grounds where of old ships were built to control the lake. One of the R.M.C. buildings is still known as the Stone Frigate. Every Canadian knows that the education given there to the cadets is a sound one, with its emphasis on mathematics, engineering and discipline; and its graduates have been distinguished all over the world in peace and war. Percy Girouard made the place famous in Egypt and South Africa, working with Kitchener; and in the Great War 982 cadets served, of whom 147 were killed or died on service. Two out of three, we are told, won decorations. In one thing (even the most loyal British subject must admit this) the R.M.C. is outdone by West Point. The uniform of the American cadets was devised long ago, when gentlemen understood how to dress, and affected neither the elaborate nor the slovenly; and Democracy has spared West Point and its uniform. In this (whatever decline private life may encourage) the cadets are beyond all comparison the best dressed men of North America. You would hardly notice even our Governor-General himself in all his glory among them. The cut-away blue coats, the gilt buttons, the white trousers silently suggest days more beautiful than ours.

§ 3. "THIS FAIR TOWN'S FACE"

But the railway station, the bridge, the forts have delayed us. It may be some slight palliation to plead that you often had in those days to wait for the train to bring you in from the junction; and at last it would arrive, ringing its bell as it went through the streets (strange sight and sound for the newcomer), and passed the City Hall. Fortifications and a battery once stood in front of the City Hall, which had been intended for a Parliament House of the United Provinces. Another blow to the picturesque and the historical was dealt; and now "tracks" and platform replace the fortifications, but serve little purpose, lying about like the obsolete tram-lines in the town itself, as if waiting for someone to sweep them up and tidy the place. It needs it. Progress has done little for Kingston; it owes all to Nature, the U.E. Loyalists, the British taxpayer, and Queen's University.

It is a strange old place, with history in all its old streets, history in their names, in their associations, in the old square stone houses. Mr Edwin Horsey has written of Ontario Street, as it is now called, and what it might tell us, if it could take a voice, of men of every race and caste, the French founder and his soldiers and priests, La Salle, Indians, *coureurs de bois*, angry colonists in arms from New York towns, Loyalists, General Rottenburg, British soldiers and navy-men, ship-builders and captains, Irish immigrants with ship-fever, and Canadians in khaki going off to serve the Empire in South Africa and Flanders. Old and new are tumbled together in strangest confusion—the old stone houses in their quiet dignity, cheek by jowl with every sort of frame-house from shack to villa, and interspersed with modern erections in red brick, some of unobtrusive monotony, others triumphs in the ornamental beyond the dreams of those who decorate wedding-cakes in sugar. All along the streets are the maples. Once planted they grow, and escape the official mind, to the great happiness of all who love beauty and like shade. There are more beautiful and impressive trees in Canada than "the maple leaf, our emblem dear", but they do not grow so quickly; so, when new streets are laid out, it is "the maple leaf for ever". The song is passing out; the French Canadian air, "O Canada", replaces it; and some day perhaps someone will write English words for "O Canada" that suggest meaning and are worthy of the music.

One feature of Kingston streets in our youth, that has vanished, was the board-walk. Flatted logs were laid parallel along the sides of the streets, and the boards were nailed down across them with huge nails; and for miles, up street and down street, you could walk on wood—with some little variation in winter, depending on the degree of care with which the snow was cleared or trodden down. It craved wary walking; and in winter, if a house overhung the board-walk, it was wise to look up as well as down. Six or eight inches of snow might lie on the roof, and day by day the heat of the house melted it a little beneath; the slight trickle of water froze, and with the days the icicle developed. In England the icicle is a dear little thing, as its diminutive name suggests; here, as the weeks passed and the process went on, it grew and grew till it reached the size and weight of a man; and when spring came on, or a premature thaw occurred, it was a real danger. One well-known Kingstonian carried an arm he could never use again, after an ice-fall from a roof. But take the board-walk on a clear winter night, when it was not buried in snow, and as you moved along it would surprise you. The shot of a pistol—well, nothing surprises us in these days of motor cycles and gramophones; but the pistol-shot in the lonely street under the stars, what was it? Just this; the boards grew old, water seeped down along the big nails, froze, thawed and froze again, the thing worked loose in time, froze up, and then your weight on the board gave it its chance and with a terrible crack it freed itself from its fetter. Your house did the same thing on a smaller scale; and if immigration laws had ever permitted the entry of ghosts, they would have enjoyed our houses. What cracks the woodwork gave off, as it cooled in the evening when the furnace-man banked the fire too early; and again when he came at six in the morning and the hot-water pipes grew hotter, and in the room over-head you heard the heavy measured tread of the burglar who was not there. We did little in burglary, though two miles away the Government provided quarters for the whole pro-fession.

Fire was for long the great danger of the Canadian town as of the forest. The dryness of the summer—Englishmen don't realize how hot "our Lady of the Snows" finds herself all summer—the increased dryness produced by the hot-air system of heating, the shingle roofs, provided endless chances for fire; and a very little carelessness was more than enough. The newcomer opened his eyes to find fire insurance two and a half times as much as in the Old Country with its wet climate and "roofs of slated hideousness". Charles Dickens once visited Kingston and touched it off in a quip: "Indeed it may be said of Kingston, that one half of it appears to be burnt down, and the other half not to be built up." In our time we had no general fire. To have been in a burning town once is enough—the horror of the sweeping smoke, the flying cinders, the noise, and your own helplessness, and what Pepys justly calls the "most horrid malicious bloody flame". In 1923 at Berkeley, California, six hundred houses were burnt in two hours; and next day the whole area lay desolate; the chimneys stood, and the front steps, and the iron bath lay tumbled in a heap of black ashes, amidst ten thousand wire nails. No, but it was bad enough at Kingston to see the wing of the hospital burning in the sunlight on the day before Christmas, with the water supply in the street frozen. Churches burnt, and were rebuilt, with the circular seating which American architects took from the theatre to brighten the house of God; it gave the choir a better chance. Nowadays this plan is being discarded for the older style.

It was a town of churches; and the historians linger over the old builders, the Reverend John Stuart, the Anglican and Loyalist, and Bishop Macdonnell of another race and communion, and the others. The Baptist Church was frankly the most hideous—like a big Punch and Judy stand in brick; but early in this century the Baptists moved out into a better building of stone. Perhaps the most attractive structure was the Church of England St George's Cathedral, to the building of which no less a person than King George IV himself contributed £1500. The Romans had the better site, easily the best in the city, and put a big barn-like church upon it; and then in the 'eighties arose their first archbishop, with a gift for the strong hand, strong drink and strong Latin. He loved to rule, and to build, and to write a resounding inscription in which the words Jacobus Vincentius Cleary were conspicuous; and his greatest achievement was the tower of St Mary's Cathedral. Two hundred feet or so it rises from that crowning site; it dominates the town; and as you approach by river, lake or highway, it is the first thing you see. One mistake the archbishop made as builder (he had other lapses that vexed his neighbours); he used the Kingston limestone, and splendid as his tower looked and still looks, the most impressive thing in Kingston, already, though it was only finished in 1889, it has given succeeding archbishops great anxiety; it is hardly a play on words to say it is an heirloom that costs much to keep up. Cleary died about 1899, a couple of years after a furious denunciation of Protestant marriage as legalized concubinage; and legends were current in the town of utterances of his adherents frank beyond the belief of posterity and its printers. His successor was a wiser and gentler man, a gentleman in fact, and not Irish.

From the church let us turn to the market. Saturday was market-day, and in summer the great square behind the City Hall was packed with the "rigs" of the country people, "buggies" and "democrats"; and Kingston thronged about them for fresh vegetables, fresh fruit, fresh poultry. Prices were not high in those days; there was no efficient cold storage, no Yankee dealers coming to buy Canadian produce to hoard it for winter prices. And sooner than take their stuff back to the country, the farm-people at the end of the day would part with it for little enough—a pair of chickens for 25 cents (not big chickens, but already respectable); a turkey in late October for 60 cents (you carried it home yourself by the legs); honey at 10 cents a section. Living was cheap and agreeable, if you took care of your clothes; for food seems always the heaviest item in domestic expenditure; but you or your wife would very commonly have to do the cooking. If you didn't like this, people would "board" you; they cooked, and you went to their houses to "eat", and the prices again were not high. To "eat", that was the word, literal, painfully literal; hence the American sign: "Drive in: Good eats". "Dinner" was at noon or 12.30; "tea" at 6 or 6.30—"high tea" as it used to be called in Scotland. Afternoon tea you sighed for in vain in those days; but civilization is winning the day, and the importance of afternoon tea in the intellectual life is being gradually recognized. Is not the spell between 5 p.m. and 7.30 p.m. admittedly the best time for intellectual work? Ask any Old Country college man. In those days, when there was tea at all in the afternoon, it would be indeed a function; a "Pink Tea", the journals would record, or a "Ten-Cent Tea" for some charity; and a list of the great ladies present would be appended. A man might be there, under special circumstances. Otherwise you needed a very good wife, if you were going to have a cup of afternoon tea.

West of the market, along the historic King Street with its old houses, one came to the City Park. It was once an artillery parade ground, but the government gave it to the city. It was planted with trees, notably elms, about 1857, and the years have made it more and more beautiful and restful. Day by day the authors of this book had to cross it on their way to Queen's. Fronting us as we entered, between the Russian guns from Sebastopol, stood the statue of Sir John Macdonald, with a sentence from one of his last speeches, which, like the trees about the statue, grows in value with the years: "A British subject I was born; a British subject I will die." And so he had died, in 1891; and with the years "manifest destiny" and Fenian raids seem forgotten across the border, and it is conceded to us that we may remain British subjects though on the North American continent. Of course that was what we intended all along to remain; yet it is a relief not to be shouted at, to quit our shackles and in freedom's name accept an alien government. President Franklin Roosevelt is even willing to protect us, which is a little too like Nicaragua status.

But we did not always think of national questions in crossing the park. One always remembers the coming of robin and grackle—the rustle of the one along the ground, the harsh note of the other from the tree; and here were the birds, and the winter was going to be over. Spring never comes in quite the same way in Britain; it is more like the bride's progress to her new home in the West of Ireland, two steps forward and one step back—sometimes even one forward and two back. But here were the robins, come to be with us after their migration—not the English robins, but thrushes with breasts as red; and they were welcome. A great old bird-man of Western Ontario has recorded that the grackle only began to come to Canada, or at any rate to the Hamilton region, in the 'sixties. He has not the yellow bill or the gladdening song of the English blackbird, and his black has a sheen of purple about it; he bullies other birds atrociously; but he too is a herald; and, when the fall comes, what a sight it is to see these birds massed in the trees, chattering over the southward flight they will take to-morrow! But it is the bird that comes North early that gives the more unforgettable happiness.

Nowadays the park and the streets have another resident. Only once do I recall seeing a black squirrel in Kingston in the old days; he was on a tree in the park and a little crowd gathered to watch him. To-day they are all about the town, as they are in the residential quarters of Toronto—quick, bright, black creatures, wonderfully attractive, bigger than the red, smaller than the grey. People who want to grow bulbs complain of them, as some people in England grumble at the blackbirds for stealing their fruit. Yet you can buy fruit and flowers in the market or at the florist's; but nowhere can you buy birds and squirrels to live with you, nor any other angelic company. Later in summer Baltimore orioles, in yellow and black uniform, and even humming-birds, came among us. Gardens have more lovers now than in old days. The American or democratic plan of having no fences is fatal to gardens; you need a fence to protect grass and flowers from your neighbour's dogs, and boys, and waste paper, and other saddening details. Still, in spite of the removal of the fences, the gardens are greatly better.

Westward again is the hospital. It took the city some years to get it, and more to be sure of it. A Female Benevolent

Society came into being in 1821 and worked for it; the Legislature made a grant of £150 toward a hospital; a site was acquired and extended. Buildings rose, but it hardly looked as if they would be a hospital. Parliament used them for some time; and by and by an Act was passed permitting the use (or lease) of the fabric to the people who were planning to start a university. But the hospital was never actually a home of Queen's College. In 1867, a year before the nadir of the college, the hospital authorities told the citizens that it was touch and go whether they could go on with their work at all; they had no funds to do it. The people rallied to them, and seventy years have seen great extensions of building and work, in the relief of suffering and the progress of medicine, and the training of doctors and nurses. When one reflects that the population in the 1830's was under 5000, and to-day after a century is little above 25,000, one feels that the town has not done badly for the development of the higher life in Canada. Archbishop Cleary contributed a marble angel to the hospital grounds to record the wickedness of the English in Ireland and the sufferings of Irish immigrants; he was induced to modify his emphasis on the former point; and Principal Grant's public address, in accepting the angel, was a masterpiece in the art of changing the subject.

Westward once more—but in Kingston the compass surprises you. There is of course the lake, the *southern* boundary here of Canada, and the main streets go up from it at right angles; so naturally they go North. A man wrote a poem about his experience with the North wind blowing down Princess Street while he had the frozen lake behind him; and then discovered that the sun towards its setting in summer shines along the street; so his North was West. But not really; for Princess Street, if you follow it, turns out to be the main motor road to Toronto which lies South West. The lake and the river in fact flow out to the North East. The parallel streets at right angles to the shore meet surprisingly; one stranger, taking a walk, found that, like Alice through the Looking-Glass coming back to the house, whatever street he tried and wherever he turned, he seemed in a few minutes to be at Chalmers Church. The fact is that the shore makes not a straight line but a considerable curve; so the parallel streets are an illusion. Still Ottawa is more confusing. Yet Canada for thousands of miles does lie to the West. So the term cannot be quite wrong.

Westward then, from the hospital and Queen's, lies a new region of residences pleasant enough in their modern way, with a fine old house looking down on the lake, Alwington. Alwington was built by the Baron de Longueuil, inheritor of a French title given by the French King to one of the great Le Moyne family and confirmed among other titles and seigniories at the Conquest. The house was the residence of the Governor till Kingston ceased to be the capital; so it too is historical.

After Alwington come Government institutions, not beautiful—though the woods of Rockwood beyond the village of Portsmouth were and perhaps are a haunt of birds. Then comes the Golf Club, the latest and finest of the golf clubs, with a magnificent new grain elevator full in front of it on the lake; and after that you reach country. Drive on, and then turn to the right, pass an odd little isolated school, built of stone, so far from anything that you wonder any children can reach it, and half a mile brings you to the Bath road. The drive to Bath is delightful if you like quiet country of our sort, farms never very flourishing perhaps and scarcely prosperous now, with constant visions of the lake and its islands and the Bay of Quinte.

Five or six miles out from Kingston, the road brings you to the village of Collins Bay. Collins, historically, was a surveyor who mapped out this part of the country. The bay is a beautiful one with wooded shores opening out southward into the lake with "The Brothers" islets over against it, and behind them the great Amherst Island and the Bay of Quinte. A little village, with a post office and store, a small church, and scattered farms, what a place it was for a quiet holiday forty years ago! Woods lay between the farms and the Grand Trunk line, and the shore road climbed a little among cedars that were a constant delight. The roads were dusty, the days long and hot, but dusk brought cool and the fireflies. Memory does not dwell in the dust, however, but clings to trees, snake-fences, birds and beasts, the friendly country people, the new baby and the books. But we have left the town behind; and, though it is always pleasant to linger in Collins Bay, we must return to our corner.

Chapter III

FRESH WATER COMMERCE

§ I. AN ISLAND IN THE UPPER ST LAWRENCE

From the days of the French explorers until the coming of
the railways the St Lawrence was the chief route through
a vast area of the New World; the early roads were feeders
of the waterways rather than their competitors. Since the
1850's the railways, and more recently the motor highways,
have carried nearly all the passengers and an increasing
share of the goods traffic. To-day, ocean travel makes the
great river well known up to Montreal; above Montreal it is
little known, though its beauty, despite deforestation and
water-power development, remains unique. And there is the
story of its trade.

The history of commerce on these great inland waters is
one of rapid changes. Places once unknown have become busy
ports, others once important must now be searched for on
map or chart. Especially is this true of those places whose
activity grew wholly out of the exploitation of the forest—
out of the export of square timber and staves, and out of
wood shipbuilding: they rose rapidly from small beginnings
to a "peak" in the 1860's and 1870's, then declined even
more rapidly. Perhaps the last of such places was Garden
Island, a little island of eighty acres in the North East corner
of Lake Ontario, two miles South of Kingston. It seems to
have been one of several islands granted by the French
Crown to the great La Salle, as part of his seigniory. Beyond
it lies the much larger and longer Wolfe Island, and beyond
that again the American channel and the New York State
shore. Here the lake is becoming river; there is a steady

current in Kingston Harbour, yet the water is open and often stormy.

Garden Island was granted by the British Crown to a retired military officer named Cameron. His first house, a two-roomed log-cabin, was in use forty years ago as a shelter for farm implements. His second house was burned in 1935. Cameron, in 1836, sold half his island to my grandfather who bought the rest of it a few years later. The new owner continued to cultivate the South West area which Cameron had cleared: the lower end of the island he put to business uses and there grew up a varied commerce, all based upon wood. The first little vessel was launched in 1841. Square timber, pine and hardwood, was made in the nearby forests and floated to the island to be rafted for the river journey to Quebec for export to Britain. It comes with a shock of surprise to recall that even Wolfe Island, that home of farmers, contributed square timber so recently. The trade expanded, a fleet of vessels (first schooners, then steamers) was built to go up the lakes to bring timber from ever further westward. Offices were opened in Quebec, a Glasgow firm acted as agents in Britain. A number of wooden paddle-steamers were built or acquired for towing the rafts and river-barges. Marine salvage was another activity. One experiment was the building of a wooden sailing-ship for salt water; her story is told in another section. In its busiest days, the little island village of employees numbered about eight hundred people, increased during the navigation season by some three hundred workers on the vessels and rafts. Many of the river-men were French-Canadians; some settled at "l'Île au Jardin" and it became bilingual. The decline of the business dates from the depression of 1873–8, though there were periodic revivals of activity.

Recalling the island as it was in the later 1890's (in my father's time) during one of these revivals of the square timber trade, one thinks first of the variety of its occupations.

The rafting was done in the sheltered water East of the island, in an area of some thirty or forty acres enclosed by wooden wharves along the shores and a series of wooden cribwork piers connected by floating timber "booms". Special machines of local invention had been developed for the rafting, which had a whole technique of its own, not seen elsewhere. The shipyard included all the traditional ancillary work in a dozen different trades. Even at this period the island was still almost wholly a wood-and-water establishment, though coal had displaced wood as fuel both afloat and ashore. In the wood-burning days, a fireman had his pay "and his ashes", which he sold to the potash makers.

The island was endlessly interesting. Besides the work in wood and metal there were special interests—the arrival of vessels from up the lakes, holds full and decks piled high with timber; the departure of the rafts; the flurry of despatching a salvage expedition. Once, when foundations were being dug for a building, a skeleton was found. An Indian? A sailor? French or British? A rusted sheath-knife was the only clue. There were trips down the river on the rafts; and longer trips up the lakes, picking up timber here and there; the slow steamers were sometimes a whole day out of sight of land. The Great Lakes are truly freshwater seas; the smallest, Lake Ontario, is about 200 miles long and equals Wales in area (7000 square miles); the largest, Lake Superior, is as big as Ireland (32,000 square miles). Familiarity with the lakes both increased and decreased the interest of one's first Atlantic crossing. The scale is very different, of course; but a landfall is a landfall, whether from fresh water or salt.

The seasons governed all the island's work; as summer waned, activity waned with it. September brought the first heavy rains; during the later autumn gales there would be steamers sheltering in the lee of the island and under the islands to the West. The seas rolling in off the lake in autumn and early winter were long and heavy; fresh water does not foam and hiss like sea-water, it is darker and more sullen under the gale. The home vessels came into winter quarters, with anchors down or chains out to the piers. There were casualties, of course—damage from stranding, sometimes loss of life. One recalls rowing a skiff, on a clear calm day after a violent gale, between the masts of a schooner towed in off the lake on her beam-ends, but still floated by her cargo of timber. Her crew were all lost. Had they been drowned trying to reach land in their "yawl-boat", or washed off the capsized vessel? No one ever knew.

Navigation closed during November, or early in December; one small steamer was kept in commission until the ice "took", usually mid-January. When the ice would bear it, a heavy traffic began between Kingston and the big islands, whose names—Wolfe, Amherst, Simcoe—recall the early days. Our island's chief part in this winter traffic was the hauling in of certain annual supplies of material, mainly for the rafting. Reconditioning of the vessels and new construction in the shipyard went on all winter, though some days of blizzard or extreme cold made outdoor work impossible. Crossing the ice in such weather was a taste of Arctic travel. The ice "went out" in April—to see the sunlight glancing again on the water was an annual joy. Presently the vessels left for "up the lakes"; the timber that had wintered at the island was got ready for the first raft; the new vessel was launched from the shipyard; the annual cycle was completed.

The last launching was in 1906, the last raft went down the rapids in 1911, all work at "the island" ceased in 1914. Twenty years of sun, storm and ice—particularly the moving ice in the spring—have almost obliterated the wooden wharves and piers that once saw so much activity. The older wooden buildings are decaying, the place is reverting to its natural state. Its commerce of eighty years lived on the cutting of trees, now the trees are gone, it is all a thing of yesterday. Steel steamers pass up and down the great river, loaded with wheat, coal, oil. But none carry timber and none "round to" at the foot of Garden Island where once stood, to guide their homing vessels, the owners' private lighthouse—a "light of other days".

§ 2. UP THE LAKES

"Log" is the curt heading of the little record: more than two thousand miles of steaming, on all five of the Great Lakes, are covered on a dozen pages of short daily entries from mid-July to mid-August of a year in the early 1890's. Captain "Abe" made me start this log and I had to write it up regularly each evening when he was doing his own; if I was too sleepy he would let me off, but not longer than the next morning. At the back of the log-book there is a record of one's small expenditures, totalling $2.03 (8s. 5½d.). It seems to indicate a sound early training in finance.

Memory holds almost no earlier impression than watching Abe's steamer and her tow-barges leaving the island on a summer evening. Across the water came the deep staccato grunts of the big steam-whistle giving the barges orders about length of tow-line, and the shrill note of the signal-whistle in the steamer's engine-room. Its last long blast meant full speed ahead; the steamer would then be opposite Abe's house at the top of the village road; he blew three long blasts of the big whistle as a farewell salute to his wife—and to the village generally, for most of the men in the three crews would be "islanders". In half an hour they passed out of sight behind Simcoe Island; this was not the regular channel, but it was ours, there were shoals but the islanders knew them. After three or four weeks they would reappear loaded with timber, unload it for rafting down to Quebec, and start off again up the lakes...when would one be old enough to be allowed to go with them?

The moment came at last. As the signal for full speed was given, one felt for the first time the strong vibration from the powerful engine, which soon became so familiar. Abe told me to blow the good-bye salute; it took all my strength, but it was worth it. Then, while the daylight lasted, a tour of the steamer: a word with the second mate on watch forward; aft to the engine-room to see the chief engineer and to check by clock and revolution-counter his statement that "she's makin' about ninety-five turns"; galley and mess-room were busy with preparations for "night-supper" at twelve o'clock when the watch changed; then right aft to see the taut slope of the nine-inch tow-line out over the taffrail down into the boiling white wake from the twelve-foot propeller; forward again to see the navigation lights set (they were oil lamps in those days); lastly into the darkening wheelhouse to see the compass-card in the light of the binnacle-lamp. Out on deck again, and the thrill of looking out for the first time over the great open lake from a steamer's deck; when the captain gave the wheelsman his compass course one felt that we were off on a great adventure.

Soon it was time to turn in. The captain's cabin, where I lived with the "old man", was directly aft of the wheelhouse. It was about fourteen feet by ten feet, its walls and ceiling were panelled with ash and walnut; it was lighted by four small windows, one on each side and two looking aft. On the port side was a built-in bunk with chart-drawers under it, the foot of the bunk was against a tiny wash-room in the corner. There was a sofa, thwartships, between this wash-room and the starboard side of the cabin, in which was the door opening out on the bow-deck. In the opposite corner from the wash-room stood the captain's desk, its great interest was the loaded revolver in one of its hiding-places.

A portrait of my grandfather was fastened to the panelling between the desk and the bunk; this steamer, then ten years old, was the last vessel he had had built on "the island", and she was his special favourite.

The noisy ritual of deck-washing got one up in time for six o'clock breakfast. Two hours later we reached Charlotte (accented on the second syllable), at the mouth of the Genessee River, the port of the city of Rochester, N.Y. There we took in bunker coal. Then out on the lake again; we arrived during the night at "Pordaloozey" (Port Dalhousie), the Lake Ontario end of the old Welland Canal. A first trip up the canal was interesting: tugs handled the tow-barges, locking through with them; the steamer went on ahead under her own power. Canalling has a technique of its own: the way of handling the lines entering and leaving the locks, the signals to passing vessels, going dead slow past dredges at work, signalling for railway and road bridges to be opened. The log says: "saw the collie that turns the bridge"; the dog and his master, the bridge-man, pushed at opposite ends of the turning-lever. And there were the filling and emptying of the locks and the working of their gates.

We had to wait some hours at Port Colborne, at the Lake Erie end of the canal, for our barges to catch us up; the log says: "we pulled clear of the breakwater at 8.15 p.m." We were on Lake Erie all the next day, for many hours of it out of sight of land, but never without sight of other vessels, for we were now among the American "upper-lakers", the great fleet of steamers for whom "the foot of the lakes" was (and still is) the port of Buffalo, N.Y. at the east end of Lake Erie. That evening there passed close to us, ablaze with electric light, one of the great fast side-wheel passenger steamers that maintained overnight services between American lake-cities—Buffalo and Cleveland, Cleveland and Detroit, Detroit and Buffalo. Early on the second morning out from

Port Colborne we dropped one of our barges near the mouth of the Detroit River to wait at anchor there while we went on to Toledo, Ohio, and left the other at that port to load oak timber. In the afternoon we picked up the anchored barge again and entered "the rivers", as the run between Lake Erie and Lake Huron is called—first the Detroit River, then Lake St Clair, then the St Clair River. "The rivers" carry a tremendously heavy traffic; they are one of the world's busiest stretches of water. And they are rich in French names —Grosse Point, Écorse, River Rouge, Point Movillé, Bois Blanc Island. This last the sailors pronounce "Bobalow"; another and larger Bois Blanc Island (in Lake Huron, near Mackinac) they call "Boy Blank". All along the Great Lakes there are these traces of the seventeenth-century pioneers, each lake has its Presqu'île, Grosse Île, Pointe au Sable.

It was blowing hard from the North, most welcome after the heat on Lake Erie; we went slowly out between Port Huron and Sarnia on to Lake Huron; then Abe hauled off to the East out of the regular traffic-lane, and anchored. The barge shortened the tow-line with her deck-winch and we lay there for some hours waiting for the wind to moderate— not that we could not have gone ahead, but Abe's object was to save fuel. We got under way during the night; I remember being wakened by the noise of the windlass getting up the anchor.

We were all the next day on Lake Huron, again out of sight of land most of the time, but passing many steamers, among them the *North Land*, one of the early twin-screw fast passenger vessels built for the upper lakes. Gulls followed us, as they do at sea, to pick up scraps of food thrown overboard. The next forenoon we called in for a few pieces of pine at a little place almost at the Straits of Mackinac, called Cheboygan. The mate alleged that the town had its name from the words of an Indian chief, when another male infant

Plate V

The Rideau Canal at Bytown (Ottawa)

arrived in his wigwam, "She boy 'gain". Our next objective
was Scott's Point, on the North shore of Lake Michigan.
There, and at two or three other nearby places, we were
busy for two days loading small lots of pine timber from the
beaches to which it had been hauled during the winter. This
"lake-shore loading" was slow and strenuous work. The
vessels anchored and lines were run ashore by our small
boats. The timber was then hauled out from shore to vessel,
a few pieces at a time, along these lines, and loaded by the
deck-winches. "Non-union" hours, from dawn to dark,
were the rule. The log records: "went ashore and cut a
couple of poles in the bush"; one of them became a private
flagstaff at the island a few weeks later.

Then back through the Straits of Mackinac—past St
Ignace, where the French Jesuits had one of their missions
and where La Salle's *Griffin* may have called on her first and
only voyage in the autumn of 1679. Lake Huron again, then
up the St Mary's River, through the big lock at Sault Ste
Marie, Michigan; there was no lock on the Canadian side in
those days. This was on a Sunday, the tenth day after leaving
the island: the log says of the American "Soo" that "everything
was going like a week-day", it records the names of several
big upper-lake steel steamers seen at close range, also that one
"saw some Indians in a canoe shooting St Mary's rapids".

And so on, out on to Lake Superior. The log confesses that
"we rolled a good deal and I was seasick". I still remember
that event: my cap blew off as I hung over the rail and I did
not miss it for a long time. At a place on the South shore of
Lake Superior (I cannot identify it), about ninety miles West
of Sault Ste Marie, we took into steamer and barge several
hundred pieces of pine timber—two busy days' work. At this
farthest of our loading-places we were about five hundred
miles from the island in a direct line and about nine hundred
miles by water.

4-2

It was some years later when I first saw the whole length of Lake Superior, the greatest of the lakes, lonely and forbidding enough even in midsummer. It never becomes warm, the very surface water remains almost ice-cold under the August sun; bad weather, gales and snowstorms come early in its high latitude. On one crossing of Lake Superior our steamer was the refuge of hundreds upon hundreds of small birds, apparently on their migratory flight. They were curiously fearless; they went into every part of the vessel, they perched on our shoulders, one could pick them up at will. They rested for an hour or two with us and went on their way.

To return: after passing the "Soo", homeward bound, we did not stop until we got back to Toledo, where we found the barge we had left there fully loaded and waiting for us. We, and the barge we had taken with us, then finished out our loads with oak timber. Our holds were full of pine, and that we were able to load oak on deck means that it was midsummer and fine weather. The islanders' euphemism, that a drunken man "had oak on deck and pine in the hold", is sufficient commentary. On the nineteenth day of the trip all three vessels were ready to start for home. On the way down Lake Erie there was "a stiff breeze and quite a heavy sea"; then we had a quiet day locking down the Welland Canal, and the log ends on the evening of the next day with the words "Expect to be home in an hour".

§ 3. THE LAUNCHING

The launching was to be on "Thursday, after dinner". Everyone on the island knew of it; there was no need for a notice on the blacksmith-shop door, where political and other announcements were tacked up. ("Blacksmith-shop telegram" was an island synonym for a rumour.) School would be closed, for no one would go, even if it were open. Only the very old and the very young were absent from the shipyard on the afternoon of a launching. The last two hours of preparation were not tiresome, they heightened anticipation, for all the men of the island had had a hand, directly or indirectly, in the building of the vessel.

Eighteen months before, "the Boss" and his foreman shipbuilder had completed their joint labours on the model. Both men would have laughed at anyone who credited them with being naval architects. They were not, but they thoroughly understood the building of wooden vessels for the island's own trade; their vessels could be picked out anywhere on the lakes, by those who were able to recognize a shipyard's "build" when they saw it. They had a look all their own, sturdy and conservative. There still went to their building, in a world that even forty years ago was increasingly mechanical, a high proportion of skilled handicraft.

Through the weeks and months, in all weathers, the sawmill had been cutting good sound oak for frames and planking. How one hated to see this clean new-cut wood hauled through November mud and rain on its way to "the red shed" to be worked at by the ship-carpenters. One watched instead the big sure-footed horses that did the hauling, especially the heaviest team, a black and a grey, driven by a voluble little French-Canadian. The blacksmiths had been turning out wrought-iron bolts and spikes; "the Boss" would not use machine-made steel spikes but insisted on small flat heads and fine-drawn points, made by hand on the anvil, one at a time, in the good old way. Bolts and spikes were driven by hand; the men always emitted a curious characteristic grunt at the end of the stroke—without it the swing and blow of the heavy long-handled hammer was not complete. And it was a more pleasant sound than the staccato blows of the pneumatic hammer which superseded it in later years.

Steadily the vessel took shape; her bows, high in the air,

became the chief feature in the island scene from all points of view. The sharp ringing sound of the caulkers' mallets succeeded the slower rhythm of the bolt and spike driving. Still later, the vessel's sides above the water-line were planed and painted. The upperworks were built; the government surveyors came and measured the new craft for tonnage and registration. Suddenly the vessel took on a new and different look, one felt that she was out of her proper element—launching day was not far off. No, there was no need to tell our island village the time of a launch—it announced itself. On "Thursday, after dinner" everyone was on hand, waiting expectantly and watching the bustle of the final preparations.

Presently there was a shouted order and the sharp, hard, hammer-blows of the first "rally" began. Four gangs of men, one on each side of each of the two lines of "ways", drove home the long rows of wooden wedges that would lift—ever so little—the weight of the vessel from the blocking on which she had been built. The blocking was then knocked away and the men moved up for the next "rally"—the last was under the bow, farthest from the water. The huge weight then rested wholly on the greased ways. Heavy ropes joined the standing and the sliding ways to check any premature movement; tackle had also been rigged to start the movement if necessary.

There was no christening or naming ceremony at our island launchings. A sharp order to cut the ropes followed the last rally. "The Boss" and his foreman watched intently a white chalk-mark drawn at right angles across the line where the sliding ways (which the vessel would carry with her) rested upon the standing ways (which would remain in their position). At first no movement at all; then the upper half of the chalk-mark was surely a *little* nearer the water than the other?... "She's moving, Tom"... "Yes, sir." The first inch took perhaps half a minute—it seemed an eternity. Then, with a cracking, squeezing sound eloquent of irresistible force, the movement suddenly increased. "There she goes!" Everybody said it at once. In a few seconds the stern pushed deep into the water, then rose as it floated. The resulting pressure under the bows, still land-borne, set the grease and oil on fire. With a final surge the new vessel floated free, leaving a great gap where for over a year she had been building. No need here for drag-chains or anchors—two miles of deep water welcomed their newest burden. Tugs took the vessel in tow and brought her round to shelter behind the island for fitting-out. Long ago, it was the custom to tow the new vessel, gaily dressed with flags, around the harbour to show her to the shipping.

There is surely no event in any other kind of work that is quite like the launching of a new vessel. A locomotive is built, steam is raised for the first time, it makes its first move; a building is completed and put into use; no one wants to see these things. A launching is a different matter. Why? Does one go only to see the slow, then faster, movement as the new creature leaves what has become a strange element for the one where her active life will be spent? Or is it a deep-seated instinct of race? After all, we come of Saxons, Danes and Norsemen; the Elizabethan seaman is the ancestor of the lake sailor; and Jacques Cartier and Samuel de Champlain are names we do not forget in Canada.

§4. A LAKE-BUILT OCEAN VESSEL

In 1875–6 the lake shipping business was at a low ebb. The schooners—particularly perhaps the timber schooners—were losing money, for the timber coves of Quebec, at the export end of the trade, were glutted with unsaleable timber. To keep the shipyard at Garden Island in being, and to try something fresh in the stagnation of lake freighting, it was decided to build a salt-water ship.

The task given to the shipyard foreman, Henry Roney, was to design and build a deep-sea vessel as large as could be got out to sea by the existing St Lawrence canals. Roney was a skilled craftsman who had been engaged some years before from among the employees of the Admiralty dockyard on Navy Bay, where the Royal Military College now is. Roney's working model is at a scale of ⅜ in. to the foot, built up of alternate layers (lifts) of black walnut and white pine. The lines of the model are not unpleasing, in spite of its being rather "beamy". The bow is slightly "clipper" and not very full, the "floor" is not too flat, the "run" is very good indeed. The stern is round.

The *Garden Island*'s dimensions were 168 feet over-all, 36 ft. 3 in. beam, 21 ft. 4 in. moulded depth. Her registered tonnage was 870, which meant a dead-weight carrying capacity of about 1150 tons. She was very stoutly built of oak and elm, fastened with iron where the sea-water would not get at the metal, and with trenails of oak or locust in the outer planking. The butts of the planks were fastened with "yellow metal" bolts; timber "ports" were framed in her bow.

Though small, the *Garden Island* was a "tall" ship, her mainmast truck was 128 ft. above the deck. Her mainyard was 76 ft. long and the mainsail 32 ft. deep. As was usual in a vessel of her size and type, she carried no "skysails", but only "royals". The standing rigging was of wire rope, the sails were of linen canvas; both materials were imported from Britain. Cotton canvas came into general use not long after this period.

But though wire rope and canvas, and probably other materials, were imported, the vessel was most thoroughly a product of "the Island". The pride of Roney as builder, and Dix as sailmaker, in their more important work, would not be greater than that of the master-painter, a Manxman named Crane, in his. There were many yarns of "old Crane's" sayings and doings; one at least is authentic, that he hired helpers from among the village boys by a method all his own. The applicant for the dignity of "pot and brush" was put on the scales and his wages set—up or down— according to variation from Crane's standard, which was 'Eye-ty pounds, tinp'nce a day".

After being surveyed and registered in Kingston, the *Garden Island* was launched on 8 May 1877. She was towed down the St Lawrence and its canals. When she reached Quebec and was seen among the many timber-ships of that date, it was plain that the dimensions forced on her by the St Lawrence canal locks gave the *Garden Island* a look of her own. She was not just the true salt-water type in her proportions; with her 36 ft. 3 in. beam, she would have been, if built at Quebec, perhaps 240 ft. long instead of 168 ft. However, her broad beam enabled her to carry her tall spars.

The fitting-out of the ship was completed as she lay at Bowen's Cove, Sillery, five miles above Quebec; Dix had come down with her to do the rigging. The *Garden Island* was then loaded with her owners' timber and started on her maiden voyage.

Her captain was Edward Zealand, a salt-water sailing-master who had been in command of lake schooners for some years. Among the crew, "before the mast", were two men who had worked at her building and rigging: Tom Brian, who later succeeded Roney as shipyard foreman at Garden Island, and George Dix, a son of the sailmaker. Brian has often told me of this voyage and how when "on the wind" the short little ship seemed to drop from under them, as the crest of a long sea boiled aft and she went down into the hollow.

The *Garden Island* reached Greenock, twenty-seven days out from Quebec, at the end of June 1877. After discharging she was docked and copper-sheathed. She was then towed down the Firth of Clyde to Ardrossan where she loaded coal for Montreal. About 1 October 1877 she sailed from Montreal for London, with wheat. She was towed down from Montreal past Quebec and cast off opposite Bic, from which point she had continuous strong westerly gales, arriving off Gravesend nineteen days out from Bic. This was her "record" voyage; the owners could hardly credit the cabled news of her arrival.

The log of the *Garden Island* is not available, but one four-cornered trip is typical. First a cargo of wheat from Montreal to Antwerp; thence to South Wales in ballast. This ballast was white sand for glass-making. The third lap was with coal from a South Wales port to Havana, Cuba; the fourth from Havana to Montreal with raw sugar.

During the whole of her first seven years the *Garden Island* ran without any insurance, escaping all damage to herself and having to pay only one solitary claim, $60 to the owners of a Portuguese ship, whose jibboom she tore out in a slight collision in an American Atlantic port.

She made her last voyage for her builders and first owners in 1883-4: coal from Troon to Colombo; in ballast from Colombo to Rangoon (she must surely have been the only vessel hailing from Kingston, Ontario, ever to enter and clear from either Colombo or Rangoon); rice from Rangoon to Glasgow. There she went into dry-dock for overhaul in the early spring of 1884, and was sold to Norwegian owners.

The new owners changed her name to *Trio*, and her registry to a Norwegian port: she was in Quebec on her lawful occasions at various times in the next eight or ten years, until the sailing vessels were ousted by the steamers from the Quebec timber-export trade. Only occasional scraps of news of the vessel reached the island for many years. She had almost been forgotten, at any rate by the younger generation, when one day the casualty lists in the English marine papers included the loss of the Norwegian barque *Trio* on the coast of Durham, near Hartlepool. This was in 1906 or 1907, in the spring, and might well have been the last news of the vessel.

But a year or two afterwards the Garden Island lake steamer *Simla* was at "the Island", and a casual sailor from her crew was sent to the sail-loft for some gear—rope or canvas or the like. The stranger's eye was caught by a coloured drawing of the *Garden Island* done by the George Dix who sailed in her on her first voyage. Asking about her, he was told by John Dix, a younger son of the original rigger of the *Garden Island* and now in charge of the loft, that she had been sold to Norwegians and renamed *Trio*. Upon this the sailor became excited, saying that he himself had seen her driven ashore, and telling a story of a two-day fight by the little ship to get sea-room in a north-east gale, while people watched her, powerless to help. Suddenly the struggle ended—the sailor could not be sure whether it was the forestay or the bobstay which parted, but the foremast came down, she fell off into the trough of the sea and was soon driven ashore, drowning most of her crew. He recalled that the coal from her cargo spurted up from the hatches as the seas broke her up.

It was an end like that of hundreds of her kind. For thirty years the little vessel was afloat, chiefly in the "Western Ocean", whose temper is shown by the fact that the "Plimsoll mark" demands the highest freeboard for the North Atlantic. Her lifetime covered the growth of the Cunarders from the little *Russia* to the *Mauretania*; she had survived into another age of ships.

But the men who were rescued from her probably shipped again as soon as they could... "I must go down to the sea again."

§ 5. "WRECKIN'"

The veteran paddle-steamer *Caspian* was feeling her way down
the St Lawrence on a foggy morning late in August, some
forty years ago. She had left Kingston at five o'clock, the
"Mail Boat" of the day, bound for Montreal—a fourteen
hours' trip, running the rapids. She had called at Clayton,
N.Y., for her American passengers at half-past six, and
was groping for her next stopping place just above "The
Narrows", the deep channel that runs for about twelve miles
in United States water through the main group of the
Thousand Islands. She got too far over to the North and
"piled up" on a shoal.

The call for help reached Garden Island towards eight
o'clock. "The Boss" had been out giving orders and getting
the expedition organized; he came in late for a hurried breakfast. I made bold to ask if I might go to the "wreck", I had
never been at one. Permission given and breakfast over, I
hurried down to "the front wharf" where two of the firm's
paddle river-tugs were taking salvage gear aboard. The big
steam-pumps and the diver's outfit would probably not be
needed, one heard, but they would be taken along as a pre-
caution. The "wreckin' lines", as the men called them, were
the chief interest for a youngster. Eleven- and fourteen-inch
lines are exciting, even though rope sizes are measured by
girth, not diameter. There was nothing equivocal about their
other dimension, each was eight hundred feet long. At last
one was to see these monsters in use.

I went in the bigger of the two tugs; the fourteen-inch line
lay in long bights on her upper deck, joyful to walk upon.
I was under the eye of "Tom", the foreman "wrecker", a
big dark Irish-Canadian, grizzled and lame, who smoked
black chewing-tobacco in a clay pipe. One learned to keep
to windward of it. I already knew every inch of the *Chieftain*;

engine-room, galley, cabins, mess-room, wheelhouse, also where it was best to stand to see the five-foot cranks of her beam-engine turning their great smooth circle. And every inch of her became more interesting because we were on our way to a "wreck".

Interest was further heightened because the "wreck" was a "Mail Boat". Though it was many years since they had carried Her Majesty's mails, they were still "Mail Boats" to all river-men. They had survived, as summer tourist carriers, from among the many steamers that once ran between Niagara or Toronto and Montreal, stopping at the little river-mouth towns along the Canadian shore of Lake Ontario and at the settlements along the St Lawrence. They were for many years the only regular link of these places with the world outside; they ran early and late, the full river season of seven months, as the freighters still do. Some of the iron vessels among them were designed and set up in Britain, on the Clyde and elsewhere, then taken to pieces and sent out to Canada by sailing ships, to be built into permanent hulls at Quebec or Montreal. Their engines and boilers were usually built in Canada, and their wooden "upperworks" always. They burned up myriads of cords of the finest hardwood as fuel, before scarcity and rising prices forced the change to coal. In spite of their light draught (for the rapids), which made them rather indifferent "sea-boats" for rough weather on the lake, they did their job competently, and maintained a regular service for freight and passengers. Many compliments upon their "good accommodations" and excellent meals may be found in letters of 1835 to 1860.

To return: we reached the *Caspian* before noon. "Tom" went all round her in a small boat, sounding; only her bow was aground and he quickly decided that the two tugs could pull her off. The big "wreckin' lines" were made fast to her, well aft; the two tugs slowly moved away, paying out the big

lines as they went. They stopped; the lines were made fast
to their tow-posts, they backed down towards the *Caspian* and
stopped again. Then, full speed ahead, the great lines
tightening and finally coming out of the water for an instant
before sagging back; the *Chieftain* listed heavily as she dragged
the big line up out of the current. The two tugs did not make
their first jerk in perfect time; the second was better, the
Caspian moved. Two or three more jerks and she floated, the
little job was done. We got back to the island towards
evening.

That of course is salvage at its lowest terms, however
exciting for a youngster to watch. "Tom" would have called
it "doin' a job by main stren'th and ignorance". But the
great river gave the island firm many a real problem of
salvage work, different altogether from salvage on sea-coasts
with their tides and gales, but difficult enough in its own way.
The current of the St Lawrence, for instance, is not a thing to
be trifled with.

The *Spartan*, another of the old "Mail Boats", once broke
a rudder-chain when she was just above Lachine Rapids. If
that chain had broken a very few minutes later, when the
steamer was nearer to the rapids or actually in them, there
would probably have been a tragedy: as it was, by quick
action, skill, and a bit of luck she was got over into shallow
water near the North shore of the river (the island of Montreal),
where she "fetched up" against rocks, broadside to the
current. The current heeled her over, the dammed-up water
poured in cataracts around bow and stern; it was a bad
situation for a moment, but she did not roll over, as was
feared. The steamer's lifeboats, aided by canoes and flat-
bottomed "chaloupes" which were poled upstream into the
eddy formed by the steamer herself, took her two hundred
passengers off safely. In the meantime the island "wreckers"
had been sent for. Two tugs, fitted with powerful deck-

machinery for strong steady pulling, were sent down and moored to the river bank about a quarter of a mile above the "wreck". Then came the real difficulty; to run the necessary lines, slanting across the heavy current, from the salvage steamers to the *Spartan*. First, a very light line was taken down by a small boat. It was a real test of skill to get this first line aboard the steamer at all, lying as she did like a great rock splitting the current and thrusting the water away from herself. But it was done. Then heavier lines and wire cables were got across. Ashore, huge sets of "tackle" were set up to aid the tugs' machinery. All lines, wires, and tackle at a job of this kind were the special care of "Cap" Dix, who worked with "Tom" as his expert in "running gear". When all was ready, after several days of strenuous and often dangerous work, the *Spartan* was slowly hauled free of the rocks and upstream to safety. She was little damaged.

Sometimes the island had to send to the rescue of its own vessels. One of the firm's lake steamers, loaded with wheat, went ashore in a fog on Long Point, a dangerous spot in Lake Ontario, fifty miles west of Kingston. I can remember well the serious unhurrying hurry of preparation for that expedition: it was fine weather, but October, and it might break at any time. One of the river-tug captains was most unwilling to take his boat out on the lake; "the Boss" told him curtly that *she* would go, whether *he* took her or not. "All right, sir", said he resignedly, in his French accent, "I know I'll be drowned, but I'll go." He went, but he died in his bed long years afterwards, for the fine weather held and the job was quickly and successfully done.

In the firm's office there were photographs of various salvage exploits. There was the raising of the *Canada*, one of the big overnight passenger boats running between Montreal and Quebec, sunk near Sorel by an ocean-going collier. Her upperworks were lost in the salvage operations, but hull, boilers and engines were recovered; the steamer was rebuilt and with a new name saw many more years of service. Another picture was of the release of the stranded bow-half of an American upper-lake steamer. The bow-half, for she had been cut in two for her trip through the canals on her way down to salt water.

Still another was of a job that I had seen myself, the salvage of the steamer *Ocean* in the heavy current near Iroquois, half-way to Montreal. I went off very casually with that expedition. Coming over from Kingston at midday on the "ferry-boat" one could see the activity that meant a "wreck" somewhere. Two tugs had started down the river; a third, with a tow-barge to be used as a lighter, was at the wharf. They were just starting as I got ashore; there was no time to pick up any "kit". All I knew, as I ran up the ladder to the barge's deck, was our destination, distant enough to mean that we could not arrive until the next day. It was a slow trip; there is something specially slow about being towed —except on the rafts, that was different! I turned in about ten o'clock in the captain's bunk but found it already occupied. I left "cimex lectularius" in possession, and went out to sleep uneasily on deck, on some tarpaulins piled against the barge's rail.

"Tom" had gone down in the first tug; when we arrived he had been at the "wreck" for some hours and had already laid his plans. The lighter was not to be used, so I went aboard one of the tugs, a new single-screw vessel. The *Ocean* lay broadside to the current, against rocks, as the *Spartan* did above Lachine rapids; the water here was quieter, and it was a less risky job, but awkward enough. "Tom" planned a combination of jerk and steady pull: two tugs were to jerk, one ahead of the other, and the third was tied up to the river bank, with gear (like that set up to free the *Spartan*) to hold any gain made by jerking. It took all day, in that swift water, to get everything rigged up. Towards evening we made our first attempt—and pulled the pawl-post out of the bow of the second tug! Repairs were made next day and we tried again. This time the cast-iron cap on the tow-post of the leading tug was broken by the terrific pinch of the three "turns" of the big line around it. Pieces of iron flew like shell-splinters, but no one was hurt; the line, however, was instantly cut by the jagged iron as it broke, and once more the gear had to be set up. At the third attempt everything held fast, but we failed to move the stranded vessel. The first engineer of the leading tug then had a useful though lawless idea; he loaded down the safety-valve till the steam-gauge showed a pressure many pounds above the legal 145. With this added power, a well-timed jerk stirred the "wreck"; the long wires of the steady-pull gear held the gain; two or three more jerks and the steamer was free. Another job finished; both this one and the rescue of the *Spartan* were typical of this kind of work, which is nearly all planning and preparation, the actual performance is usually brief.

The islanders liked "wreckin'". I do not know why they never used the official word salvage, but they did not; as soon as a vessel was in trouble enough to need help she was a "wreck" until she was freed. The men got extra pay for "wreckin'", for it was very hard work, with long and irregular hours; on the other hand it was more exciting than their day-to-day jobs. Wrecks were one of the islanders' stock subjects for discussion and argument. This was especially true of the occasional failure, for the firm more than once attempted the impossible. "Tom had ought to 've tackled her like this", an old-timer would say, as he produced a bit of chalk to illustrate his theory by a rough diagram. I have never heard that any of our islanders followed the alleged custom of the early Scilly islanders, and actually hoped, even prayed, for wrecks. No, but they welcomed them, all the same!

§ 6. A SKIPPER OF THE GREAT LAKES

The Great Lakes have been called "the most crowded water-way in the world". It is said that four times as much tonnage passes through the locks at Sault Ste Marie in a lake season of eight months as through the Suez Canal in a full year.

This great volume of trade is of quite recent growth. I remember hearing, in the 1890's, old Captain Muir of Port Dalhousie tell of the dismasting in a Lake Ontario storm, in 1837, of a little schooner in which he was mate. The vessel was worked into the mouth of the nearest river, on the New York State shore; new spars were cut in the bush, set, and rigged. When they reached Kingston, at the foot of the lake, they heard of the death of William the Fourth and the accession of Queen Victoria. Thirty, or even forty, years later, lake navigation was still on a small scale, both as to the size and the number of vessels engaged in it. In the 1870's the building of steamers began, and in the next thirty or forty years, ending with 1915 to 1925, there was enormous expansion. It was chiefly an American expansion, but Canada had her share in it, especially of late years. The largest lake steamer afloat is Canadian built and owned—the *Lemoyne*.

Abe Malone, born in our village, and for forty years the senior captain of the Garden Island lake schooners and steamers, saw in his lifetime of fresh-water sailing all the changes implied in the growth that has been outlined. He has told me that he remembered, as a small boy in the 1850's, the old-timers of that day shaking their heads over the newest Garden Island schooner, the *London*—they thought her too big to be handled safely on the lakes. The *London* carried about 400 tons dead-weight; when Abe retired in 1912 there were whole fleets of steamers on the upper lakes carrying from 5000 to 8000 tons. These big steamers can now come down into Lake Ontario through the enlarged Welland Canal—in the summer of 1932 I stood almost on the very spot where the little *London* was built, and watched through glasses the *Lemoyne* arriving with a cargo of 12,000 tons at the great grain-elevator, three miles away on the mainland. So much for the rapid growth.

There are two fundamental differences between navigation on the Great Lakes and at sea; both arise from the relatively restricted area of the lakes. One is that on the lakes all navigation is on compass courses and by "dead reckoning"; positions are never determined by observation with instruments, as at sea. The other is that a lake vessel must be thought of as always on a lee shore; at sea, a ship may run before a gale for days, but a few hours is the most that can be hoped for on the lakes. In the autumn of 1913 a dozen steamers were caught in the lower end of Lake Huron in this way—there were no survivors, nor any salvage, over two hundred men were lost. But that is a unique example of this danger.

The typical lake captain is a man who has come up from the lower deck. There are no training ships for lake officers: they get their training in the University of Hard Knocks— though the knocks are not so hard, and have never been, as those one reads of in novels of seafaring. There are two reasons for this: first, the scarcity of men when lake shipping was developing; second, the short trips—it was easy to "quit", or even to desert if necessary. A man begins as deckhand, becomes watchman, then wheelsman, gets his mate's papers and finally his master's certificate. He has no knowledge of navigation in its salt-water sense, his knowledge is rather that of the highly specialized technique of the lakes— of navigating big steamers in crowded waters, day and night, and of using every minute of time to advantage. The cardinal sin on the lakes is losing time.

5-2

"Old Abe", for he shared this name with a famous American, belonged to an earlier school. He began as apprentice in a timber-schooner and became a captain in sail. From the *Oriental*, a two-masted fore-and-aft schooner in which he had been master for some years, he went in 1884 into the Garden Island firm's first lake steamer, a wooden vessel built in their own yard. She was towed via the Welland Canal to Cleveland, Ohio, on Lake Erie, to have her engines and boilers installed; there was then no Canadian lake port equipped to supply them. As other and larger steamers were built by his owners, he commanded each in turn when she "came out"; they were engaged chiefly in the timber trade.

Of hard-working thrifty Ulster stock, Abe saved enough money to buy eight of the traditional "sixty-four shares" in his first command. His interest in her was transferred to his steamer commands, one after another; to pay the increasing cost he continued to turn in his share of the profits. There were many tales, some true and others invented by jealous rivals of softer fibre, about the extreme parsimony by which Abe got together enough money to buy his first share, and to increase it. Certainly there was no luxury, as I know from experience, where he was in command. He told me himself of buying cheaply, in a little American port, a tub or two of very excellent butter, but the risk of its too speedy consumption worried him. When it first appeared—officers and men messed together—Abe tasted it ostentatiously and remarked on the skill of the slick Yankee, who could make oleomargarine taste like real butter. Whereupon a greasy stoker, tasting it from his knife, alleged that he would "ha' knowed it anywheres for oleo". It lasted much longer than usual. But Abe did not always guess right, in his attempts to increase his share of the profits. For instance: a cargo of big timber was relatively easier to handle than one of small— fewer pieces, less stowage, and the vessel would carry more cubic feet. So, the first time that Abe, as steamer captain, went with two tow-barges to load from a boom full of one maker's timber, he made his crew bring the biggest timber to the steamer. But, when the vessels were credited with their freights—so many pieces at the average size of the lot—the steamer got credit for less than the amount she had carried. For years afterwards, in all such cases, it was noticed that Abe's steamer was always loaded with the smallest timber. He "got his own back", many times over. A more pleasant trait was Captain Abe's love of reading, he was particularly fond of Shakespeare. My first visit to the theatre, as a small boy, was with him. We saw Robert Mantell in *Othello*, and I can remember my host, who was word-perfect in his favourite plays, accompanying some of the actors, *sotto voce*, in their lines.

But these things are by the way. The skipper's real job, on fresh or salt water, is the successful handling of his ship, especially in difficulties. In October of 1893 Abe left Fort William, on Lake Superior, in his first steamer, then nine years old. He had two barges in tow, all three vessels were fully loaded with wheat, the speed would be about six knots. A bad Nor'-Nor'-West blow came on, casualties were reported; Abe was overdue at Sault Ste Marie and his vessels were posted "missing". A day passed, and they were reported lost with all hands. Next day he telegraphed to Garden Island that he had arrived at the Sault, all well. A week later he was discharging at the grain-elevators in Kingston, and told "the Boss" his story. The gale had caught him well out on Lake Superior, he could only run for it. He found himself unable to make Whitefish Point, above the Sault, and was being driven on the South shore further West. The only possible shelter he could reach—with disaster if he missed it—was the lee of an out-of-the-way island where years before he had once loaded pine timber. He "made it" and waited for the gale to blow itself out. No one in any of the three crews, except "old Abe", knew where they had been! There was perhaps no other lake-captain of his time, certainly there are none to-day, who besides knowing intimately all the regular lanes of traffic, had also been in every kind of odd place picking up timber—at river-mouths, in bays, and lying off open beaches.

His quick resource in difficulty showed itself once when I was with him in his second steamer, the *India*. We went aground while going slowly through fog, at six o'clock on a Sunday morning, near Port Colborne, at the Lake Erie end of the Welland Canal. Within half an hour, or very little more, he had his tow-barge alongside, clear of the shoal he was on (it was calm summer weather), and was lightering his cargo of iron ore on to her deck. He sent for a tug, and within eight or ten hours we were afloat again, with no damage and the minimum of cost.

In the late autumn of 1901, Abe was running down Lake Huron from the Sault, bound for Goderich with wheat, in the *India*. He had no tow-barge this time. They sighted a barge loaded with pulpwood, rolling in the trough of the sea; it was blowing hard from the North West. Abe brought his steamer close in, blew his whistle repeatedly, but there was no response—the vessel had been abandoned. The glass was falling, the wind increasing; Abe would have left her, judging that she was leaking badly and was floated only by her cargo. But Abe's crew "mutinied", they scented easy money. They took charge of the *India*, the first mate and two men went on board the derelict and made Abe take her in tow. When they arrived off Goderich the weather was so bad that though the steamer could have gone in alone she could not take the barge with her—it was a question of speed when entering between the piers. Abe let go both anchors, night came on, it blew a heavy gale. In the morning there was no sign of the derelict (except pulpwood strewn along the shore), and the three men in her were lost. In the inquiry before the Dominion Wreck Commissioner, later on, Abe and his owners were exonerated from all responsibility.

All these dangers, and the skilled courage that meets them, are little realized by Canadians and Americans, even by those who live along the Great Lakes. This is not surprising. It is a long time since the lakes were the usual route for passengers, and, when they were, the vessels of the period had to lay up early; they could not navigate in all weathers. For many years the only lake passenger traffic has been in the summer months, on steamers ever more luxurious; aboard them danger seems very remote. Lake yachtsmen? Yes, but they too are out only in the three summer months. The only men who really know the lakes are the comparatively few who sail them for a livelihood; and they *do* know them. I was once with Abe in the *India*, coming down Lake Superior in a thin haze on a fine August day; we began to hear the fog-horn on Whitefish Point. I commented on its mournful, monotonous sound. "My boy", said Abe quickly, "if you were coming down here in November, in a gale o' wind with snow, you'd think it was the best music you'd ever heard!" For snow is perhaps the lake sailor's greatest menace; it is just as blinding as fog and it usually comes with high winds, not with calm, as fog does.

"Old Abe" has been dead these many years, but innumerable pictures of him survive in memory. The earliest is personal: his hoisting me hand over hand, with a line under my arms, from a small boat to the after-deck of his first steamer—a great adventure at six years old! I see him loading timber, indistinguishable in garb from his mates and crew—exchanging greetings, from the bridge, with the lockmasters in the Welland Canal—in blue shore-going kit, reporting at a Custom House—giving the mate his orders before "turning in"—coming into Garden Island in December after the last trip of the season, muffled to the eyes, his steamer coated with ice.

The dark water "smokes" with the cold, there is ice along the piers—it is time to "lay up".

Chapter IV

THE RAFT

§ 1. EMPIRE AND TIMBER

There was a legend that Nelson won the battle of Trafalgar
with ships built of the oaks which Englishmen had planted in
the reign of Charles II as a result of reading John Evelyn's
Sylva. That book was the first outstanding plea in English for
deliberate reforestation. Readers of Henry Grey Graham's
Social Life in Scotland will remember his account of the passion
for planting trees that swept over the great landlords of
Scotland in the eighteenth century. Some of them planted
millions, it is said. Yet one of the difficulties of the century
was the want of wood for fuel at once in industry, in the
kitchen, in the parlour, for building purposes and for shipping. Civilized man is the enemy everywhere of forest; he
must hack it down to get arable land. In French Canada
grants of land were made with the condition that the land
must be promptly cleared. With the growth of industry
(particularly iron and steel) and the call for shipping, England was stripped of her forests, and timber became a
problem.

Whether Evelyn's book gave Nelson his fleet or not, fleets
for war, for commerce, for passenger service, were more and
more needed, and some large part of Britain's foreign policy
turned on timber supplies. The Baltic must be kept open at
all costs to make sure of timber from Sweden and Russia. In
the Mediterranean area there were negotiations with Ali
Pasha, the tyrant of Janina, to get timber from his Albanian
forests. As far afield as Burma timber was sought, and
merchantmen were built of teak at Rangoon. The trade with

Canada included a constant demand on the Maritimes for shipping timber. Let it be remembered that (as Evelyn saw) timber fit for shipbuilding grows slowly and needs to be replaced, that planting long seemed needless in Canada, and that the general use of iron for building the hulls of ships only dates from the middle of the nineteenth century, and it will be seen at once what significance attached to the timber trade of the Great Lakes. It has passed away; and British shipbuilders have used British Columbia fir and Georgia pine; the deck of the liner must be free from knots. Before long they will be looking out for new forests to devastate. "To-morrow to fresh woods," as Milton put it.

The amazing influence of deforestation on climate, on agriculture, on the change of air and of soil, lies perhaps away from our present theme. But it must not be forgotten. At all events for some decades, after the wars were over, our corner of the Empire was vitally bound to Britain by the timber trade: every summer, and all summer, the timber passed down the St Lawrence on its way to Liverpool, Belfast and Glasgow—and Garden Island had a big share in the traffic.

§ 2. DOWN THE GREAT RIVER

The white man's attack on the forests of North America goes back almost to the beginnings of his life on the continent. Its most ruthless phase dates from about a century ago. At first the timber was "made" along the shores of the great river and its branches, and floated to Quebec for export to Britain. As the country near these waters was settled and cleared, the timber was cut farther and farther back from their shores; the same process went on along the Great Lakes and their tributary rivers. During the later years of this trade a large part of the timber came into various lake ports by railway; Toronto and Hamilton used to handle considerable quantities of pine and hardwood timber from the western peninsula of

Ontario. This rail-and-water business developed until finally pine timber came into Duluth (at the head of Lake Superior) from as far West as Idaho, and oak into Toledo, Ohio, from as far South as West Virginia, Kentucky and Tennessee. All of this timber was carried down the lakes in vessels to the bases of the rafting industry in the neighbourhood of Kingston and there "rafted up" to go down the St Lawrence to Quebec for export to Great Britain.

For some fifteen years before the rafting ceased (in 1914) Garden Island was the only survivor of these rafting establishments. The island had developed its own special methods. I can remember well the rafts built by its last competitor (at Collins Bay, West of Kingston)—they were in a general way the same as the island's rafts, but there were essential differences.

Timber was also sent down the Ottawa River into the St Lawrence below Montreal Island, and on to Quebec, but the Ottawa raft was a different species, built for different conditions. Most of the Ottawa rapids were passed by sloping sluices or runways called "slides"; the Ottawa "cribs" which slid smoothly down these great wooden troughs could not safely have run the St Lawrence rapids. The "drams" of the St Lawrence rafts were of a much sturdier construction. It may be that this stronger type of raft was evolved in dealing with sinking timber like oak, for all the Ottawa timber was pine. Nor was rafting on the Ottawa a distinct trade, as it was on the St Lawrence. An Ottawa raft was usually one man's timber and remained in his hands from the bush right through to Quebec; on the St Lawrence, especially in later years, rafting was a forwarding business for various owners of timber in widely separated places, in both Canada and the United States.

In eastern North America the word "timber" has a specific meaning, it is not a general term as it is in Britain.

Timber, with us, means tree-trunks either partly squared, with broad slightly rounded corners, called "wanes", left where the bark has been cut away, or else squared down until the corners are sharp. The biggest and best of the white pine was always cut "waney"; the rest of it, and nearly all the oak, elm and other timber, was cut square.

And now to follow the timber from its unloading out of the lake vessels at Garden Island until its arrival at Quebec. The loose timber was made up into "drams"; the "dram" was the unit of the St Lawrence raft. A pine or elm dram was in three tiers, or layers, called bottom, cross-tier and top-tier: an oak dram had only one, for even with some pine to keep it reasonably buoyant it floated just level with the water. The best grade of oak will sink; but, as the quality of the timber lowered with deforestation, a progressively higher proportion of it floated, and less pine was needed in rafting it. The reader may be more familiar with this difference in the quality of oak than he supposes. For example, he may have wondered why furniture makers have for some years seemed so fond of dark finishes on oak. One reason at any rate is that dark finishes hide the more open grain, and the blemishes, of inferior wood.

It would be impossible, except at considerable length and with the help of many diagrams and photographs, to describe in detail the building of a dram. The men who worked at it were nearly all French-Canadians; their expert labour and steam power were both required, the former especially in the tying of the hundreds of "withes" (small birch saplings crushed and softened between steam-rollers) that held together the bottom tier of timber and the framework of the dram. From the tough elastic nature of the withes and their being evenly and snugly tied, a really extraordinary strength was developed in the whole fabric. On it was loaded the cross-tier, on that again the top-tier, which was not always a

Plate VI

At the island; withing bottom tier of pine dram;
stern of lake timber-vessel at left

Tom Abram, a typical "Indian" (half-breed) raftsman

complete one. The finished dram of pine, containing 600 to 700 pieces, was a floating island of wood, able to resist great shocks and even greater strains. A dram was always 60 feet wide; the length varied from 250 to 350 feet. Thus a raft of eight drams, two abreast, was 120 feet wide and 1000 to 1400 feet long, and covered a greater water area than the *Queen Mary*—does it suggest the vast reaches of the St Lawrence, to think of such a huge thing navigating them?

On one of the drams was built a little wooden cabin containing four sleeping bunks, a cook-stove and a table; in it lived Aimé Guerin the Garden Island firm's headman on their rafts, the foreman of the raft, the cook—and the occasional guests. On another dram was the men's cabin, with eight bunks, where the rest of the crew lived. In later years canvas cabins were used. The equipment known as a "raft-kit" was a varied lot of gear: windlass, anchor, chain, sails, a couple of hundred oars 30 feet long (cut with the axe from the same material that was used in the framework of the drams) for steering in the rapids, rope, pikepoles, axes, augers, crowbars, lanterns, a boat to carry a dozen to twenty men, a smaller boat, the cook's outfit, blankets. The food supplies were simple: salt pork, bread, hardtack, potatoes, dried peas and beans, dried fruit. The staple drink was strong green tea without sugar or milk; it was made by putting the tea into cold water and bringing it to the boil. A substantial sum of money, five to eight hundred dollars, was carried on each raft, chiefly to pay the extra men who helped in the rapids. The money was shoved into the straw of the foreman's tick and left there quite unguarded. "Hold-ups" were unknown.

Given a fine summer day—and in retrospect a raft seems always to have left Garden Island on a fine afternoon—it will easily be understood that the last hours of preparation were an interesting time. The ordered confusion of getting all the gear aboard, the half-guessed secrets of the boxes and bags of "grub", the scents of the clean pine timber in the sun, of the raw wood of the cabins, and of the fresh straw in the bunks—the shouts in French—and finally the arrival of the towing steamer, the wash from her paddle-wheels running over the edge of the raft as she stopped alongside it. Presently the tow-line was made fast to the raft, the steamer went slowly ahead until she had paid out 600 feet of line, stopped while the line was made fast to her tow-post—the engine gong was heard again, the big line tightened, and the raft started "with the stealth of a bad habit"—or of a train leaving Paddington.

Progress was very slow indeed until the current in the narrower waters of the Thousand Islands began to be felt. Little was done the first evening beyond setting navigation lights (one white light on each corner of the raft) and making things snug for the night. After six o'clock breakfast next morning there was plenty of activity. Masts were put up, and sails set if the wind was right. At each end of each dram were built rowlocks and footholds for the rowers, or more correctly steersmen, in the rapids. For the "passenger", life on the raft was very leisurely and pleasant. Visitors often came aboard and went a few miles with us; one of them, at least, thought rather of the forest than the timber—for Will Carleton, the American poet, called the rafts "the funeral marches of the trees". Sometimes, when the right men were in the crew, there would be singing of French-Canadian songs, in the evening. Our raftsmen were not so picturesque as the "log-drivers" of fiction: their usual kit was high leather boots with short caulks in the soles, trousers tucked into them and held up by belt or a bit of rope, often a heavy woollen shirt even in midsummer, a coloured neckerchief and battered felt hat.

The raft's best running time in summer, from Kingston to Montreal (175 miles), was three days. Leaving one evening, the raft would reach Prescott (60 miles) late the next evening and tie up at Windmill Point below the town. (The first rapid was near, and a raft could not navigate at night except in quiet water.) It would run the first small rapids, and the Long Sault, during the second day, and reach St Zotique near the foot of Lake St Francis (140 miles) in the evening or during the night. With a very early start on the third day, the raft would get through the four rapids of the Coteau run by 9 or 10 o'clock, go down Lake St Louis, run Lachine rapids in the late afternoon and reach Montreal early in the evening. This ideal schedule presumes fine and moderately calm weather; any other wind than the prevailing South and South West breeze usually meant tying up and waiting for a change; for example, northerly winds made it impossible to run Coteau or Lachine.

Running the rapids was the hardest work for the crew, and the chief interest of the trip for the occasional passengers. It is well worth while to go down the rapids in a passenger steamer, but from a dram of timber one saw the wild water at close range, and felt its power. It is as if the steamer went *over* the rapids and the dram went *through* them. In fact an oak dram, almost awash even in still water, went "through" literally. An oak dram had a platform built on it for the rowers to climb up on, and when it was in the roughest water of a rapid these men on their perch were all that could be seen of it. The first two rapids, the Galops below Prescott and Rapide Plat above Morrisburg, are mild—mild, that is, as compared with the others. The raft went through them without being separated into its several drams, and with the steamer towing all the time.

Below Rapide Plat the steamer and raft made quick progress in the strong current until, above Aultsville (90 miles), the Long Sault pilots and their men, some fifty or so, began to come aboard the raft. These pilots were English-speaking and lived in and about Aultsville: the men were a mixed lot; a few Indians from the St Regis reserve, men from the river farms on both the Ontario and New York State shores. One well-known figure was the schoolmaster, who always made the run through the Sault and rowed an oar. He even taught on the raft, if he could find a victim who had not been forewarned. I remember one hot July afternoon hearing him explain the composition of the Milky Way to a Queen's professor (Adam Shortt), who was a guest on the raft. This Long Sault crowd understood little French; Richard Dafoe, the senior pilot who took down the cabin-dram, spoke none at all and in his dealings with Aimé Guerin had to have an interpreter—one did not always give "Rich" an exact translation of what Aimé said about him when things were not going just right.

The timber drams did not run the North Sault, where the passenger steamer goes, but were separated out in a long line (by dropping them one after another as the steamer towed the raft) above Cat Island, keeping to the South of Long Sault Island, in American water. This was a very pretty and little-known channel, full of bends, with beautifully wooded banks. It took expert use of the long oars at bow and stern to make the dram take the turns. At the foot of Long Sault Island, and farther downstream than the main North Sault rapids, the drams went through the only sharp "pitch" of the South Sault. The drams were then reassembled: the pilots and extra men were paid off and went ashore at Cornwall (115 miles). From this point on, both shores of the river are Canadian. The raft went on down through the islands and out on to Lake St Francis, or Coteau Lake as the river-men call it, and reached St Zotique late in the afternoon.

Early the next morning, perhaps an hour before sunrise, the drams were again strung out in single file in charge of a new set of pilots and men, French-Canadians this time. The four rapids of the Coteau run lie in the various channels among the uninhabited and almost inaccessible islands between Lake St Francis and Lake St Louis. Very beautiful those wooded islands were (a morning chorus of birdsong came from their dense green as we floated past); they gave some little idea of what all the shores of the great river may have been like a century and a half ago. The drams were steered over to the North and went through the first rapid (Coteau) near the village of Coteau du Lac; there was a distinct sensation of dropping over a ledge, in the descent of Coteau. Then, after a long drift in smooth but fast water, the drams went through Cedars rapids. At the foot of them, along the South shore of the river, is the "Chute aux Bouleaux", perhaps the roughest water in all the rapids, but neither timber drams nor steamers had to go through it. Then, after another drift, we passed through the Split Rock (Roche Fondue); in it, as in Coteau and Cedars, the drams took a different channel from that used by steamers, but in the fourth and last rapid of the Coteau run, the Cascades, boat and drams took the same channel. Below Cascades Point and Cascades Island the drams were reassembled, the pilots and extra men went ashore, and the raft went on down Lake St Louis.

To digress for a moment, for Cascades Point and Island have a special importance. Those vast settling-basins, the Great Lakes, eliminate almost all silt from their waters before they leave for the sea, down the St Lawrence. The lakes, again, act as storage-basins—there is no spring freshet on the St Lawrence. In a general way the levels of both lakes and river are fairly constant; nevertheless there are long-swing variations in their levels, which have been observed for a century or more and for which it is even yet difficult to account. The water was high in 1918, then, over a period of years up to 1928, the levels of Lake Ontario and the St Lawrence fell steadily and alarmingly; doubtless, said all

Canadians (and many Americans) along both shores, it was due to the Chicago drainage-canal, the reversal of the flow of the Chicago River—drawing off Lake Michigan water and running it into the Mississippi. They forgot, or did not know, that the lowest water in Lake Ontario and the St Lawrence had been in 1895, before the Chicago affair began. Then, in 1929, without any warning, lake and river rose higher than they had been for many many years; wharves were submerged and much damage done. So, either way, what becomes of the "Chicago" argument? By 1935 the water was lower than even in 1895—and still no one knows why. Whatever its level may be, the water of the upper St Lawrence is clear—clearer in October than in April, of course—but generally speaking it is always clear.

At Cascades Point, then, the blue St Lawrence receives the first of the brown water of the Ottawa River—for a short distance a fairly sharp line can be seen between blue and brown, but soon the great river loses the brilliant colour and clearness of its upper reaches. The Ottawa drains an immense region (80,000 square miles) and pours its waters into the St Lawrence by three mouths; two, separated by Île Perrot, at the South West corner of the great triangle of Montreal Island, the third at its eastern end, below the City of Montreal.

But we were starting down Lake St Louis, which the river-men call Lachine Lake. With a fair wind the raft in a few hours neared Lachine, and the third set of pilots and men came aboard; in this lot were a good many Indians from the nearby Caughnawaga reserve on the South side of the river. (Caughnawaga is an old Indian settlement, founded by the French Catholic missionaries for their Iroquois converts— who were dreaded as much as any pagan Indians by the outlying English colonists.) It was a tradition that the leading dram must run Lachine rapids under an Indian pilot. The senior of them, a picturesque, silent veteran known to the

Plate VII

Early morning mist, Long Sault Rapids

In main "pitch" of Coteau Rapids; note the "downhill" slope
of the dram

French raftsmen as " Michel", was said to be of pure Indian blood; he wore his long black hair coiled in plaits about his head.

The most competent Lachine pilot was not an Indian, but a French-Canadian, Baptiste "Jean-Marie", who in deference to custom piloted the second dram. "Jean-Marie's" real name was Couillard; the local usage—is it perhaps an old French one?—was to replace a common surname by a man's parents' names, hyphenated. "Jean-Marie" was a tall man, of rather slight build, very quiet and reserved; like many of his people he made Ontario men of equal station in life seem rather uncouth. Once I was with a raft that stopped for Sunday at the mouth of the Chateauguay River where it falls into Lake St Louis—except in an emergency the rafts did not run any of the rapids on Sunday. "Jean-Marie's" house was a mile or two up the Chateauguay; he invited me and a younger brother to come and have a meal with him. We went, and, in spite of protests, our host put me at the head of his table; as son and grandson of the two men for whom he had been piloting in Lachine for thirty years, that was my place, he insisted. So I made my first attempt at carving a joint; our host and his wife waited on us.

Another interesting figure in the little world of the Lachine rapids, forty years ago, was Louis Jackson, the Indian who piloted the towing steamer—a different job altogether from piloting a dram of timber. Jackson was enormously fat, he shaded himself from the summer sun under a big cotton parasol—an odd figure among the hard-bitten raftsmen. But only old Aimé Guerin dared make a joke about his appearance, for he was a great man among his own people. He had been a leader in the party of "voyageurs" who were recruited in eastern Canada for the Wolseley expedition of 1882, to work their boats up the Nile, particularly up the cataracts. The late Dr W. H. Drummond has told the story of these "voyageurs" in his own pleasant vein, in his poem "Maxime Labelle", one of the best in the collection published as *The Habitant*.

But to return to the running of Lachine: once more the drams were towed clear of one another, above the C.P.R. bridge, and began the quick drift of three miles to the main "pitch" of the rapids. Below the bridge the river opened out ahead of us—a mile wide, deceptively smooth. It would be interesting to know how the technique of guiding the heavy unwieldy drams into Lachine rapids was gradually evolved. A steamer answers her helm quickly, a dram did not—but it had to find the same channel, of only a few hundred feet width, through the mile-wide barrier of rocks and foaming water that showed its white line from shore to shore, far ahead. There are no buoys or other aids, the pilots steered by their own private landmarks and "by the look of the water".

The towing steamer went on ahead: through field-glasses one could see her rolling and twisting in the main "pitch" a mile or more ahead of our leading dram. From time to time old Michel signalled silently for a few strokes of the long steering-oars at bow and stern. A glance at the shore showed that we were gaining speed—great eddies and swirls appeared on the water. Straight ahead, and ever nearer, the long line of the white, leaping, menacing crests of the great waves of the rapids glinted in the sun. Far beyond was smooth water again—but at a much lower level, for we saw only the towing steamer's smoke—she was hidden under the "hill" down which we were to follow her.

Presently the long dram undulated over the first smooth rounded waves of the rapids, a moment more and we had fairly entered. As the dram hit the first big waves of the sharper descent the steersmen hauled in their oars and ran back to escape the water as it boiled over the bow of the dram, whose whole fabric bent and strained to conform to the long

Plate VIII

Steering into Lachine Rapids, Île au Heron in background

Main "pitch" of Lachine Rapids; the rocky islet (centre) can be seen at the right in photograph above

waves of the rapids—we dashed down the main "pitch" in what seemed no more than a few seconds. There was a curious illusion that the great barely submerged rocks were rushing upstream as we passed them; the heavy timber bumped and thudded underfoot, the water spurted up in great jets as the sides of two pieces of it struck flat together. It is an unforgettable experience.

Occasionally things went wrong. I was once on a dram that turned "end for end" in Lachine. There are two sharp turns in the channel through Lachine rapids, first right, then left. If a dram entered properly, it made the turns properly— it could scarcely help doing so in that terrific rush of water. But this dram had got out of the pilot's control just above the rapids, it swung off to the left and entered the channel cornerwise instead of head-on. The "sheer", or swing, continued until in the middle of the roughest water the length of the dram was across the current—for an instant or two it was a highly dangerous situation. But the swing went on and we came out stern first, without any damage except that some pieces of the top tier of timber (on which we stood) had floated off; they were recovered below the rapids. Utter helplessness is the chief recollection of that wild run; one had a feeling of being in the grip of overwhelming elemental force.

But, good run or bad, it was soon over; the waiting steamer picked up her charges once more and towed them on down the great river. At Montreal the Lachine pilots and their men were landed. The raft's time from Montreal to Quebec (165 miles) was two to four days, a quiet lazy trip if all went well, but there was always the chance of bad weather on Lake St Peter, which is some thirty miles long by fifteen miles wide. It is a shallow lake (except the dredged channel for ocean steamers) and even moderate winds quickly raise a nasty sea on it. Or there might be a heavy East wind when the raft reached tide-water (not salt water, that begins forty miles below Quebec). An easterly blow with a strong flood tide often caused a good deal of anxiety, and sometimes accidents, but the vast majority of the rafts were finally swung safely in on the tail of an ebb-tide at the piers of the timber coves above Sillery Point, five miles West of Quebec.

On the ebb-tide of the night of 12th–13th September 1759 Wolfe's little army slipped down from Cap Rouge and passed this same Sillery Point and its French batteries, to land at l'Anse du Foulon, a couple of miles further downstream. That spot has been "Wolfe's Cove" ever since, and only recently was it defaced by a great steamship quay.

The Garden Island rafts were landed at Timmony's Cove. Some of the drams might stay there, usually most of them had to be delivered elsewhere—to Indian Cove, Bridgewater, New Liverpool, Bowen's, or Lower Sillery. The steamer could control a dram only for an hour or two at high or low water, so that sometimes it took two or three tides before the distribution was complete. The raft-crew were then paid off at the island firm's office in St Peter Street, Quebec.

The "raft-kit" was taken on board the towing steamer to go back up the river to the island; the wood cabins and the framework of the drams became the prey of the cove-men whose work it was to break up the raft and prepare the timber for export to Britain. In the great days of the square timber trade, 1850 to 1870, there would be scores of sailing ships loading timber in the Quebec area, from ten miles above the city down to some five miles below it. The quantity of timber decreased, the sailing ships disappeared. Tramp steamers replaced them at first, then cargo space in regular liners replaced the tramps. The whole trade has become a memory, except that small quantities of timber still go by rail direct to the steamer's side.

The timber itself outlasted the rafts. Years after the St

Plate IX

Nearing the foot of Lachine Rapids

A few miles above Quebec; towing steamer almost hidden by a sail

Lawrence rafting ceased, one could see, along the south-east coast of England, groynes built of rock-elm timber, and find a link with the great river in deciphering the worn but familiar bushmarks and culler's marks still legible upon their solid sides.

§ 3. LE VIEUX AIMÉ

The words mean "Old Man Aimé", not "the beloved old man", for he was the terror of slackers, and more often feared than loved. Aimé Guerin was for thirty-four years the head-man on the Garden Island rafts. By his natural ability and industry he had emerged, while still in his early forties, from among the hundreds of French-Canadians who were then working in the picturesque trade of rafting. It was whispered that when he was put in charge of our rafts all theft of timber from them suddenly ceased. The unspoken and unworthy suggestion was that Guerin had been a successful timber thief and knew how to cope with the breed.

When I first knew him, Aimé Guerin was approaching sixty, but he looked more like forty-five. He was of full average height, broad-shouldered and strongly built; his head and features were boldly modelled, particularly the forehead and the aquiline nose. The mouth was rather wide and inclined to severity of expression; his dark skin, more and more tanned as the summer passed, contrasted happily with the blue cotton shirt he habitually wore. His keen brown eyes were quick to narrow down threateningly as he gave a curt order or dealt faithfully with incompetence, but they also smiled easily—he loved his joke. "Vous avez l'air trop sérieux, m'sieu'", he often said to me.

Guerin's river-work was seasonal. He spent half the year, or more, on his farm near Laprairie, six miles South West of Montreal, across the river. A letter, dictated to one of his family, for he had had little schooling—no great loss, perhaps, to a man so naturally competent—a letter would arrive at "l'Île au Jardin" in the spring, to announce his coming on a stated day, usually towards the end of April. The letter might close with a sentiment such as "Je suis en bonne santé et préparé à bien travailler". His arrival at the island was a sure sign that the summer's rush had begun.

At the island, Aimé was not responsible for the making up of the rafts, though he knew all about that now lost art. His work began when the raft left for Quebec, in tow of a light-draught paddle steamer. Each became to him "ma cage"— *my* raft—as soon as he went on it, and it *was* his, while he was in charge. (It will be noted that the word "radeau" was not used, a St Lawrence raft was always "une cage".) Guerin's responsibility was chiefly the first half of the trip, to Montreal; still more he was responsible for the hundred miles from Prescott to Montreal, in which the rapids lie—eight of them, each with its own difficulties and dangers, and culminating in the wild descent of Lachine.

When things went well "le vieux" ruled with a light hand, but if a pilot tried to use more men than Aimé thought necessary, or if a dram got out of the channel and was damaged by bumping over the rocks, or if the captain of the towing steamer made a false move—then the culprit felt the weight of his wrath. Aimé had almost no English, but he had a wonderful store of French invective, often salted with comments on the ancestry and habits of his victim. "Crapaud!" and "front noir!" were among his mildest epithets: his favourite execration was to call the offender "bout d'maudit". I do not know the etymology of this phrase: M. André Siegfried suggested, in answer to a question, that it might be a contraction of "bout d'homme maudit" or "damned runt". At any rate both "bout d'maudit" and "bout d'enfer" became nicknames for old Aimé, in the mouths of those who had suffered.

In spite of his long experience, and his natural boldness and resource in difficulties, Aimé never took the rapids lightly—

least of all Lachine. Before entering Lachine rapids the old man always knelt down on the timber to tell his beads, and many of the men followed his example. Not without reason, for it was a fast, crooked and treacherous run, the scene sometimes of serious accident and even loss of life.

When the drams had been reassembled below Lachine rapids, and the pilots and their men had been paid, it was the cook's duty to shave the old man, preparatory to his going ashore at Montreal. This was sometimes an exciting performance. The old man always sat where he could watch what was going on—I have seen him leap to his feet, with one side of his face hidden in lather, and rush to the bow of the raft to shout orders to the towing steamer. Disdaining the aid of a megaphone, he always made himself heard and understood above the noise of the steamer's paddles or of escaping steam, even at seemingly impossible distances.

From a point about opposite his own village of Laprairie, Aimé would have himself rowed on ahead of the raft (with some final shouted instructions to captain and pilot as he slowly passed the towing steamer) under Victoria Bridge and into Montreal Harbour. He landed near the Bonsecours Market; as a devout Roman Catholic he usually went first into Bonsecours Church to give thanks for another safe passage of the rapids. From the church he made for his "pied-à-terre", the little Hôtel Riendeau in Jacques Cartier Square, where "M. Guerin" was always received with the deference due to a competent veteran engaged in a unique job of work. From his hotel he would telegraph his arrival and ask for news of the next raft; he might get back up to the island, or perhaps join the raft only at Prescott or Brockville. In busy seasons he made from twenty-five to thirty trips during the summer: he knew every mile of the river, above Montreal—lesser souls than he were left in charge of the rafts for the quieter journey from Montreal to Quebec.

Through the last years of the rafting the old man fought

doggedly on: for himself against advancing years, for his employer against increasing difficulties with men and new obstructions in the river—power-developments, bridges and the like. He died in the summer of 1909, at his home near Laprairie, only a few days after landing his last raft safely at Montreal. One remembers him most vividly as a man of action, but he was more than that. To competence, diligence and thrift he added very shrewd opinions on the affairs of the day. And he had imagination: Aimé happened to be on Garden Island one summer afternoon when fire broke out in the dome of the fine old stone City Hall in Kingston. "The Boss" was watching the fire (sympathetically) through glasses, across the two miles of water, but it was Aimé who demanded action. "Il nous faut nous montrer, m'sieu'— mais oui!" he said. So a tug was sent over and her pumps were in large part the means of checking the fire and saving the building. Moreover, Aimé had a full share of Gallic urbanity; his ease of manner in scenes far removed from raft or farm was in marked contrast to the usual diffidence of the Anglo-Saxon of equivalent social standing. It would be interesting to know who his ancestors were, among the early French immigrants into Canada.

It is perhaps dangerous, in the altered conditions of to-day, to trust overmuch one's memory of the ideal bond between employer and employed that united "the Boss" to "le vieux Aimé". But I believe that there can have been very little exaggeration in Aimé's statement to me, in his old age, that "the Boss" had never said a harsh word to him—and certainly he was trusted utterly in his job of river work. No sane person doubts the usefulness of modern social legislation, of Labour Ministries, of associations of employers and of employed—but, in the light of the mutual loyalty and regard that this gallant old French-Canadian and his employer had for each other, one cannot help feeling that, in their case at least, "the former days were better than these".

Plate X

Dram running Lachine Rapids

Chapter V

LIFE ON THE ISLAND

§ 1. FOLKS AND THEIR JOBS

Though the island still had a vigorous and strongly individual life, it could be seen even forty years ago that its activity would not survive indefinitely. Decline, due chiefly to the depletion of the forests but also to the competition of steel steamers and the railways, had set in long before I knew the place. A few of the men were conscious of this decline, and tried to reassure themselves. "Tom", the foreman ship-builder and "wrecker", once put it to me, as he puffed the evil blue smoke from the chewing-tobacco in his clay pipe, that, "when 'the Governor' died in '84, some of the crowd here thought the place would close up—when we got back from buryin' him, 'the Boss' said 'Hurrah! boys!'—and we've been goin' on ever since." Knowing my father and his feeling for *his* father, I cannot help doubting at times whether "Tom" was quoting "the Boss" quite exactly. It takes a Boswell to carry an anecdote. The work *had* gone on, but on a smaller scale, and in the face of ever-increasing difficulties.

Most of the men gave small thought to these things. They were secure in their jobs, there was employment for all of them throughout the year. At times, when regular work was slack in the winter, work was "made" for men whose special skill was essential in the summer rush. The permanent workers fell into three groups: first, the senior raftsmen who directed the seasonal workers in the rafting and whose winter work was repairing wharves or rafting-gear and helping as labourers in the shipyard; second, the ship-carpenters and others who worked at the building and repair of vessels; third, the lake and river sailors and engineers. The rafting and wooden shipbuilding were the more obviously declining activities, and in the last thirty years of the business most of the island boys as they left school went into the third group, because from it they could expect to go on to other employers if necessary. Many of them found better jobs, there were "graduates" from the island vessels all up and down the lakes; one became manager of a steel shipbuilding firm at a Georgian Bay port, others went into American employment, some afloat, some ashore.

In the summer there were various paid jobs for active boys. The smaller youngsters used to "go pickin' old iron", as it was called, which meant that they gathered up lost bolts, spikes and other oddments, either ashore or in shallow water. The boys brought them to the foreman blacksmith and were paid with an order on the store at the rate of twenty-five cents a hundred pounds. The line between "old" iron and iron picked up too close to the actual work of shipbuilding was not too finely drawn by some of the boys, but old "Andy" had a sharp eye. He kept the too new iron, but he did not weight it in for payment. Older boys worked at "tallying" the timber as it was unloaded from the vessels, they helped to measure the timber, they operated the steam-winches used in the unloading and rafting. This last was the usual apprenticeship for those who went on to be steamer engineers.

All the regular workers in our island village, except the school-teacher and the farmer, were directly in the firm's employ. Even the Customs Officer was a Government servant for only part of his time. Nevertheless, there were other occupations. For instance "Red Jim" left his ordinary work at the call of duty and became our constable. At far-separated moments of excitement he made an arrest—perhaps a drunken raftsman—under the direction of "the Boss" in his official capacity as Reeve. One of the ship-carpenters became the barber in his off-time; "Shaver" Kennedy could be seen in his tiny garden on a summer evening, busy with his customers, his steel-rimmed spectacles hanging low on his nose. From time to time he turned away for the tobacco-chewer's necessary relief. Another of the ship-carpenters used to build skiffs, after hours; he sold or rented them to the other villagers.

The tenant-farmer "up at the head" was really our dairyman; he grew a few vegetables, but his crops were chiefly feed for his little herd of cows. Early each morning his high two-wheeled cart came down the road, drawn by a small brown mare. The farmer never got down from his cart to serve his customers; like all monopolists he made them come to him. A flat-toned bell summoned the housewife or her messenger, the jug was handed up to be filled from the tall cans with a long-handled dipper. In the winter the farmer had another special job: he was required to provide and drive a daily "stage" over to Kingston and back, across the ice. The "stage" was a long box with two bob-sleighs under it and with planks laid across it for seats; it was hauled by two horses—usually at a walk. It was the winter equivalent of the ferry-boat, and the fare was the same. Many of the thrifty islanders preferred to walk, unless the weather was bad.

On the whole, the islanders were a most contented lot, very unpromising material for the labour agitator. Wages were not high, but they were adequate because living was cheap. The firm charged merely nominal rents, about a dollar a week, for the houses; their general store was more a convenience to themselves and to the employees than a part of the business expected to show a profit. Probably it ought to have shown a profit; there was a wicked criticism of "the Boss" and his uncle, made by a hard-drinking and very candid employee, to the effect that they had been "teachin' Sunday School for fifty years and never raised an island boy honest enough to run the store". The islanders had some special small advantages as members of their little community. For instance, the ordinary wastage from the rafting and shipbuilding provided nearly all their wood for fuel, free of charge. With wood-ashes always on hand, the housewife often made her own soft-soap. There was free fishing, easily available; the annual catch must have been a considerable addition to the island diet. The crews of the firm's vessels had access, during the seven months' navigation season, to the shops of American lake and river ports, where they could buy anything that they might find cheaper or better in the United States, and bring it home free of duty. The men on the river-steamers brought quantities of cheap French-Canadian tobacco and potatoes to the island. At times, no doubt, various small items of the firm's property found their way (especially from the vessels) into the households of the less scrupulous. It was even said that a former islander, a cynical Manxman, had described the place as "a small island in the St Lawrence River inhabited by thieves". Which was probably a slanderous exaggeration, though one must remember the young iron-pickers and their attempts to fool old "Andy".

At any rate it is certain that the islanders who still survive from the dispersal of the village population look back with pleasure and satisfaction to the island life. As one old-timer, exiled to Toronto, put it: "I'm glad I didn't spend my workin' days in a city. At Garden Island, now, you saw the weather and the water—you could get on a boat and go somewhere." So you could, and city amenities are poor compensation for that freedom.

Boyhood recollections of the island are pleasantly varied; the rafting, the saw-mill, machine shop, boiler shop, black-smiths at their forges, the shipbuilding. It was a delight, on a dark cold December afternoon, to climb the narrow stair, its handrail a canvas-wrapped rope, to the sail-loft. A coal stove warmed it, oil lamps hung from wires running the length of the low ceiling. There was a pleasant scent of waxed sewing-twine, new manilla rope, tarred rope. The head sailmaker, a Welshman, had been round the Horn, sometimes he would talk from out his canvas billows.

I have a relic of the sail-loft—a ten-inch hardwood sheave with brass bushings, marked "TAYLOR, OCT. 1792" and stamped with the "broad arrow". It came from Admiralty stores in the Navy Yard near Kingston, which were sold when the Rush-Bagot treaty ended the maintenance of naval vessels on the Great Lakes. That heavy dark-brown disc of wood has a curious power of evoking sight and scent of "the Loft"—and of the vanished life of Garden Island.

§ 2. THE SCHOOL-HOUSE

The strap was a real weapon of offence, it had been cut from a roll of thick rubber belting. The tall thin schoolmaster always carried it doubled up in the inside breast pocket of his coat. The coat bulged in an ugly threatening fashion; the strap seemed ready to leap out of its own accord at any moment and get to work. One memory of this is vivid—the wholesale strapping of late-comers who had lingered watching a too interesting noon-day fire. The schoolmaster exhausted himself over the job, he dropped the strap at one point in its long progress. Opponents of corporal punishment will be duly outraged to hear that this man was soon afterwards made principal of a small school in Kingston, and thence promoted to a bigger one, and that in 1935 he was given an honorary LL.D. by Queen's University, in recognition of his lifelong devotion to boys. But the great strapping is an isolated recollection, school memories as a whole go with quite other scenes. The island school-house links itself with memories of various meetings, and chiefly with Sunday services.

The school-house was a plain rectangular frame building, one storey high, its length parallel to the village street. On its roof-ridge there was an open bell-cupola with elaborate Victorian mouldings, and brackets cut with the jigsaw. The walls and cupola were whitewashed, the roof had the pleasant grey of well-weathered cedar shingles.

There were three school-rooms. The central one, the scene of the future LL.D.'s outburst of strapping and of all my other memories of the place, took up the middle two-thirds of the building. Its walls and ceiling were of varnished pine boards. The ceiling was carried up into the roof; at the top of the walls, instead of the usual ceiling joist, there was a row of iron tie-rods from which the lamps hung. In one corner was a big wood-stove, in another stood a harmonium. The desks were of solid oak, with slatted seats, superlatively uncomfortable in their own right and with the added discomfort, as one grew older, that they were spaced to suit children.

From one of these desks, as a small boy, I first heard that devastating person the "lecturer and entertainer". I remember that he caught imaginary flies against the blackboard and that he made a terrible pun with "music" and "mew-sick". He told the story of the tramp who had been given a wedge of pie and asked for a fork to eat it with. "Just you go along a bit further", said the housewife, "and you'll find a fork in the road." One worried over that; if the woman had seen a fork lying in the road, why had she not picked it up?

The school-house was sometimes used by campaign speakers for political meetings. Liberal speakers could come if they cared to, but whether in the Liberal interest or the Conservative, the meetings were purely *pro forma*. Only the men had votes in those days and they wisely voted as "the Boss" did—Conservative. A Liberal vote in the island ballot-

box meant that there was a newcomer in the village who had
not yet fully learned our traditions.

Sunday School at three o'clock was a fixed thing in our
village week; most of the Protestant children were sent to it,
some of their mothers and fathers also came. One stout
bearded man, a ship-carpenter on week-days, used to spread
his handkerchief on the floor to save his decent Sunday blue,
before he knelt to lead in prayer. The collection of coppers
was taken in a little box, said to be of teak and to have come
from India; the grooves for its long-lost sliding cover made a
useful grip for the small collector's thumb. Dogs often came
in at the open door in summer, looking for their young
masters: we saw the Catholic youngsters as they passed up
and down the village street—one wondered why they did not
have to go to Sunday School.

Sunday evening services were an institution of greater
interest. There was no church in our village, morning wor-
shippers went chiefly to Wolfe Island, where there were
Catholic, Anglican, Presbyterian and Methodist charges.
A few went to the city churches in Kingston. Our evening
service at seven o'clock was conducted on alternate Sundays
by the Anglican rector and the Presbyterian minister from
Wolfe Island. We youngsters sat well forward, near a window;
if the clergyman had not arrived we watched for him as he
came along. In the autumn he was sometimes late, coming in
drenched from his crossing in a small skiff. The Presbyterian
minister used to go straight to the platform, adjust the
table-lamp to his liking, and begin his service. But the
Anglican disappeared into the smaller schoolroom as an
ordinary civilian carrying a bag, and reappeared presently,
clad in his vestments. We all rose as he began "Dearly
beloved brethren...". He used to go through the whole of
Evening Prayer—how long the Psalms sometimes were!
We "Free Church" youngsters listened for our favourites

among his mannerisms; especially for one or two places in the Creed, and for his way of saying "...Queen Victoria...and all the Royal Fam'ly".

On Anglican Sundays the harmonium was helped out by a violinist and a small choir. The bass depended chiefly upon an Englishman who was not a member of the violinist's choir, though they counted on his voice. He was said to have been a paid chorister in London, years before: in our village he was the Customs Officer who attended to the entry and clearance papers of the firm's vessels. He used to write with a pen whose handle was a tube of yellow glass; he held it bit-wise in his teeth as he used a blotter or moved his papers about. I can still hear Dick's deep bass; my first consciousness of part-singing was his voice in the tune "Rutherford", especially the first notes of its fifth line. On Presbyterian evenings, when we had neither violin nor choir, Dick's great voice was the main support of the singing. The collection was taken up on a pair of grey agate-ware plates with red baize glued down to their flat central part—vessels much superior to the teak box of Sunday School, we thought them. Not a phrase remains to me from any sermon heard in youth in the old school-house—what survives is the contrast of the sounds of two styles, the droning smoothness of the Anglican voice and the harshness of the Presbyterian.

Whichever it might be, we finally got to the benediction—then homeward down the stony village road through the chill blowy darkness of an autumn evening into warmth and the soft yellow light of the oil-lamps that flickered as the door was opened and shut again. And so to bed—to the sounds of the wind in the trees, the waves running along the beach, and a lake steamer's whistle in the distance.

§ 3. THE OLD STORE

One begins to be an island veteran, if he can remember the old store, for it burned down in September 1897. I had gone back to school about a week before the fire occurred; three months later the new store, in an adapted building close by, seemed a most unworthy successor to the old. Let us forget it, and recall instead the old, one-storeyed, red-painted frame building that sprawled at the foot of the slope at the extreme East corner of the island, like some amphibian stopped in its progress from land to water. The beach line ran under it; about three-fourths of its area rested on the land, and one-fourth on the wooden crib-work of the wharves which extended out beyond it on two sides and seemed to hold it from sliding off the island.

Its two doors faced West; an unmarked one to the left led into the butcher's domain and the areas beyond, to the right was the main door with its two signs—STORE and POST OFFICE V.R. Entering it, you were in a room occupying about a quarter of the building; its rough wood floor had settled down until it followed the slope of the ground under it. At the left was the shop-counter and at one end of it, as you came in, was the post office. Behind this were the telegraph instrument and the telephone, a real telephone that reached out to Kingston and the world beyond. On the wall near it there was still to be seen the primitive telephone that had once been connected to its duplicate in the firm's office; they had been set up in the late 'seventies when the first telephones were described in the newspapers.

The store was a division of the island firm's business. Two men worked in it; in addition to their store duties the senior of them was postmaster and the other a telegraph operator. The butcher was also supposed to be under the senior man's orders, actually he went his own way. The customers were a

7-2

varied lot: small youngsters on errands from home or spending their own coppers, housewives, steamer and barge captains, raftsmen, ship-carpenters, older boys buying their first chewing-tobacco, younger boys getting fishing tackle. On busy days in summer most of the floor in front of the counter was covered with piles of goods ready to go "up the road" to the village houses or to be taken out in small boats to the vessels or "the raft".

From the rear of this busy place one got through into the rest of the store. Straight ahead was a small room where were dry-goods, earthenware and glassware; off it again to the left was a still smaller room where boots and shoes were kept. These two rooms were a quiet inactive backwater, a survival from the days when the village had been larger and the islanders' access to the shops in Kingston difficult and irregular.

Turning to the left at the end of the counter, instead of going on into these back rooms, one went through into the butcher's shop; along one side of it were shelves, back to back with those behind the counter in the main store. From these shelves were sold some bulky commodities that properly belonged in the main store but had been crowded out by lack of space. One of these was flour in bags. There were two brands, "Gem" and "Bijou"; the butcher gave the first a hard "G" and pronounced the second "*By*-joe". "The Deacon", as the butcher was called (not to his face), stood behind his great wood chopping-block, a steel hanging from his waist in the orthodox fashion. He used to whet his knife and cut thin little shavings of round-steak for the boys; telling us that raw meat, well peppered, would stick to our ribs. In the ice-room he had joints of beef; there was also fresh pork, but never any mutton. Smoked hams and bacon hung from the beams—"the Deacon" did the smoking and pickling of the firm's supplies, and very proud he was of his curing. Opened barrels of his salt pork stood at hand—how lovingly "the Deacon" looked at the pale dripping cuts as he lifted them out of the brine!

Beyond the butcher's shop there was a dark region where one seldom penetrated. Were there some heavy goods stored there—rolls of wire, kegs of nails? It is difficult to recall the place, though two things survive in memory—the darkness and the sound of the water lapping and gurgling on the hidden beach under the flooring. It seemed an eerie place, the warm sunshine out-of-doors was very good, after a visit "in back".

Also opening off the butcher's shop, to the right as one came in from the main store, was the paint-and-oil room, with its rows of barrels. One barrel of each oil was set up on its side and fitted with a spigot for filling the big metal measures: coal-oil for lighting, and various other oils for the firm's steamers and the machinery on the island. Here also one heard the water under the floor; but this room was well lighted and it sounded quite different. In this oil-soaked place a fire had been discovered and quickly put out, some years before the blaze that wiped out the building. I remember watching men clearing up the debris and starting repairs. That fire had a very interesting origin, one wondered about it. How did "spontaneous combustion" do its fell work? At any rate, after he had mastered the correct sound of its many syllables, it made an interesting phrase for an eight-year-old to repeat to himself—"spon*tane*ous com*bus*tion!"

§ 4. BOY AND BASS

The island is set in a wide irregular area of water, fourteen square miles or more. An opening to the South West shows a sky-and-water horizon far out over the great lake; and from the South West comes the prevailing summer wind. It

usually rises and goes down with the sun. The water is often
rough during the day; early morning (with the two hours
before sunset for second choice) is the best time for fishing,
which is always from a boat, with bait—the black bass does
not take a fly in these deep clear waters.

Sunrise in early August, before the "daylight saving" era,
was about five o'clock. A boy of fourteen looked out sleepily
from a West window in the half-light; it was dead calm,
rather warm, and hazy. Instantly he was wide awake, for it
was the perfect fishing weather that comes all too seldom.
Dressing hurriedly, the boy stole through the sleeping house
and down the back-stair into the kitchen with its big wood-
stove and its three windows looking across two miles of water
to Kingston and Fort Henry, their limestone walls white in
the level light. He took a few biscuits from a tin, eating the
first as he crossed the wet grass to the boathouse. In it were
two clinker-built skiffs: one of sixteen feet for two pairs of
oars, the other a twelve-footer, rather wide and flat, fitted for
one pair only—an ideal little craft to fish from alone, especially
when standing up.

The boy's simple preparations were a well-worn, pleasant
routine. Into the smaller boat went oars, fish-box under the
thwart, landing net, the little box of spare tackle. Then, with
half its length out over the stern and with butt and reel
resting on the bottom-boards, he put in his chief treasure, an
ancient lancewood rod. Its priceless tip had been twice
mended—by "Cap" Dix, the sailmaker—and there was no
second one. He shoved the skiff out of the boathouse and
down the runway till the stern was in the water. Finally, the
bait—his share of minnows taken in a seine the day before by
himself and one or two of the village boys. He went to the
spot where he kept the minnow-pail hanging quietly under
water, hauled it up, poured off some water, opened it, threw
out one or two dead minnows, admiring the liveliness of the

others. Locking back the cover, he carried the pail to the skiff and set it on the bottom-boards, well aft.

He glanced quickly over his gear and pushed off the skiff, jumping in over the bow, a hand on each gunwale, as she floated. He shipped the oars (the old-fashioned kind with a hole to take the pin set in the gunwale) and started up the island shore, south-westward. After a minute or two, the tall flagstaff behind his father's house came into line with the high sheer-legs, made of two eighty-foot pine mast-timbers, that stood at the East end of the island. It was the boy's own discovery that this "range" led over the big shoal off the head of the island, where in midsummer, and later, the morning fishing was often good. Wood-smoke from the village houses told of breakfast for men who must be at work at seven o'clock or earlier, dogs could be heard, there were black shadows along the shore. But the young angler's eye was on the weather—the hazy sky, the dead calm. Would it hold for an hour or so, or would the breeze come early? After a quarter of an hour's steady pulling, he rowed more quietly: he was nearing the shoal and he believed the old-timers' saying, that the bass did not like the surface disturbed by oars. He watched overside, suddenly the first big boulders rose through the dark clear water—he rowed still more quietly until the skiff was well over the easterly end of the shoal. Against the yellowish rocky bottom fish could be seen moving lazily—any bass? Yes, there were two—one was a "good one", it was exciting to see them.

The oars came in and were tucked well forward out of the way. The boy picked up his rod, loosed the hook from a cross-bar of the reel—the reel clicked sharply in the still morning air as he pulled out three or four feet of line. Laying the rod across the gunwales of the skiff, he chose out a minnow and passed the small hook through its gills. Rod in hand again, he stood up and cast towards the deepening water at the edge of the shoal. The light line, very slightly weighted above the short leader, slowly carried the shining minnow out of sight. With some twenty feet of line out, he reeled it very slowly taut, then a little more, a little more again, just enough to keep it clear of the bottom. The black bass of these waters will sometimes strike strongly, but is much more often a stealthy nibbler, and one must feel carefully for the first touch. Sometimes nothing can be felt, and the first sign is the movement of the line through the water. Seeing this sign, the boy gave the fish more line, then more, until the bait had been carried about thirty feet; he steadied himself, struck— and missed! He reeled in, a fresh minnow needed. Another cast in the same direction, a longer and more careful wait, then the joy of the solid resistance that meant a "good one". He put on a slight strain, the boat began to slip ever so little past the boulders of the bottom. The boy let the fish pull, getting the line straight over the stern to give choice of sides for using the net. He increased the strain, and began to talk to the fish, half aloud. He got in some line, then with a sudden rush the bass jumped clear—would he get off? No, still on, fighting. More line came in, another jump, then a minute or two of close-in work—the boy could see two or three other bass near the one he was playing. He shortened the line right down as the fish tired, brought him close and at the second try netted him. "Three pounds, p'r'aps", the boy said, half aloud. He trembled a little with excitement.

A good start, but the next three or four fish were only perch —"bait-stealers", the boy called them. Using an oar as a paddle, he took the skiff out to the edge of the shoal again. He caught two fighting bass, but they were under the ten-inch limit and were returned to the water. The boy looked at the weather; the sun was now well up and the haze had thinned out, but there was still not a breath of wind—how long would it last? He landed another "good one", and, as the netted fish touched the bottom-boards of the skiff the boy saw that the hook was free—it was his greatest thrill, to know that only by keeping the right strain had he got him. When there were six bass in the fish-box, it seemed just possible that the then legal dozen might be taken before breakfast. He hooked another, but lost him; then suddenly there came the morning breeze. At once the skiff began to drift and in a minute or two was moving rapidly in the rippling water, the haze cleared off, the ideal conditions had gone.

For the first time, the boy looked at his watch—quarter-past seven, he felt hungry. He rowed home, down the wind, munching his last biscuit. The skiff was hauled out, the gear put away, the minnow-pail hung back in its place. He cut a thin straight two-foot branch from a small ash and trimmed the twigs from it, except an inch of the lowest one to act as a stop. He ran the branch through the gills of his six bass, the biggest one on top, of course. After a brief swim from the boathouse pier he dressed quickly, then doused his catch in the water to improve its appearance. There was a scent of coffee as he passed the kitchen on his way round the West corner of the house to the open door of the dining-room. With elaborate carelessness the boy dropped his fish on the grass in full sight of the first breakfasters. As he greeted his mother and sat down, a younger brother got up and went out. He stared at the fish for a moment, then bent over to see them better. "Take me out some day?" he asked as he came in again. "A'right", answered the boy thickly, his mouth full of ambrosial bacon and toast.

§ 5. "THE HALL"

The interior of "The Hall" was a mystery. It was locked up in the daytime, when small boys are abroad on their lawful and unlawful occasions. The outside of the place was familiar enough—a one-storeyed frame building at the top of the village road, a bit larger than a pair of the village houses and painted, as some of them were, in two shades of brown. Over the door in its North end there was a sign, "Mechanics Institute". In the 1890's an Act of Her Majesty's Ontario legislature changed this sign to "Public Library", but the place remained "The Hall", whatever its official name, as long as the village and its commerce continued in being.

Each weekday there came into the firm's office, down at the foot of the island, a variety of daily newspapers; on some days there were weeklies also, with pictures in them. Most of these papers bore the pencilled letters "G.I.M.I." and they continued to bear them long after "M.I." ought to have been "P.L." These papers were put into a deep drawer behind and under the office counter, to be conveyed at the end of the day up the road to "The Hall". Not always on the day they arrived; by some *jus primae lectionis* certain papers used to cross the road to the "Big House" for a few hours, or overnight, before they went on to their destination. This custom gave us youngsters our first acquaintance with various illustrated weeklies, English and American.

Gradually one came to know "The Hall" at first hand. As the village workmen's free club, it was sacred to them, but one had to go there from time to time for different reasons, so that its appearance in its usual and unusual activities became familiar. The interior was a single long room; books lined the walls across one end and down one side, except where a single window broke them. Off the opposite side there was an alcove, its floor was a little above the general level and it held a half-grown billiard table. The opposite end had no bookshelves, in it were two windows, one each side of the entrance. On the walls were "portraits" of Queen Victoria and Lord Palmerston, photographs of the island's vessels, and a map or two. Four or five tables, lit by oil-lamps hanging above them, were strewn with newspapers and periodicals.

The room was at its best on a cold December evening, after the lake and river vessels were laid up for the winter and the islanders were all at home again. Gossips gathered around the big coal-stove, readers around the tables. The air, thick with tobacco smoke, carried the low murmur of voices and the click of billiard balls. More serious use of the place was made by men who were taking from the shelves the books on navigation or engineering which would help them with their winter's work toward examinations for higher certificates. The firm took a good deal of trouble to keep these technical books up-to-date, and supplemented the Government's library grants to do so.

Accessions to "The Hall's" shelves used to pass through the office, like the daily supply of newspapers. The choice of books was rather haphazard, perhaps, but a lot of very good things found their way in from year to year. The place could boast some interesting and surprising first editions, and on one occasion a Queen's professor found in "The Hall" a book on Canadian political history that he had failed to find in any other library, even in the archives at Ottawa.

In the roof-space over "The Hall" there was for many years a duly authorized Lodge of the A.F. and A.M. It was reached by a steep ladder-like stair outside the building. "The Boss" was not a Mason, and I know nothing of the activity of "the Craft" in the village. No doubt it had some influence, for one recalls that long ago the "square, compass and G" was to be seen painted on the stern of certain of the island vessels, just below the name and port of hail.

"The Hall's" chief official function was at elections, when it was always the polling-place. We youngsters liked to look at the voters' list, posted up according to law, usually in the store and on the door of the blacksmith-shop. The voters' addresses were nearly all given as on "Broadway", which was the Government's high-sounding name for the village road.

Not all the Christian names were familiar, for some of the men had almost lost theirs and were known only as "Crow" or "Swampy" or "Rooster". Their occupations, on the contrary, were always just as one knew them to be—raftsman, sailor, teamster, engineer, ship-carpenter. "The Boss" was listed as "merchant". Our island boasted one "gentleman", an ancient of no occupation whose two stepsons gave him a home.

In municipal elections the proceedings in "The Hall" were just a little reminiscent of "pocket borough" politics, without their violence. "The Boss" was the perennial Reeve of the village, he and the Council (who were really his own nominees from among his employees) were always returned unopposed. And if all the villages of Ontario had had their affairs as well managed as ours were, fewer of them would be in financial distress to-day. There is much to be said for the easy yoke of an enlightened paternal dictatorship.

§ 6. ON THE FERRY-BOAT

"Who owns all these bags?" shouted old George the purser. His question was always the same, though on a townward trip his word "bags" might apply to cattle, sheep, wagon-loads of hay, piles of cheese-boxes, market-baskets—and on a return trip to barrels of sugar, sides of beef, boxes of groceries, farm machinery, empty wagons. The purser worked his way slowly through this varied freight on the bow-deck of the *Pierrepont*, then along the crowded stuffy alleyways that smelt of engine-oil and the cooking in the crew's quarters down below, aft into the "cabin" where the farmers' wives gathered, then up to the promenade deck. He collected fares and freight charges in cash, then went to his little office on the main deck where he could be seen counting the money. We youngsters were a little afraid of old George, perhaps because of the loud severity with which he met the farmers' arguments against his charges. All the rest of the crew were our very good friends; particularly Jim Allen the captain, who sometimes invited us into his wheelhouse. The tiny place was painted a cool green—the bell-pulls to the engine-room, the compass-box, the lever for blowing the whistle, all invited comparison with their equivalents in the island's steamers.

Jim Allen's name recalls a story—a little story, but part of a very big one. His family had lived at Cape Vincent, a village on the New York State shore ten miles South from Kingston. One evening his father told Jim to take their skiff, after dark, and row along the shore into the mouth of a certain creek where there was an old boathouse at which he was to stop. He was on no account to make any noise; a man would meet him there, and he was to take him across to Wolfe Island. When he reached the place the boy could see no one. But keener eyes were on the watch, for presently a negro came furtively out of the bushes and got silently into the skiff. Silently the boy rowed across the wide river in the summer night. The skiff grated ashore, and as they got out the negro spoke: "Boy, is this Canada?" and when he heard that it was, he knelt and kissed the stones of the beach. For this was in the days of the "Underground Railway", when fugitive slaves were not safe even in the Northern States—but now between the negro and his pursuers stood the British Empire. He was free.

The *Pierrepont* was owned by a Kingston firm that had contracts with the Post Office for the carrying of the mails and with the island townships for a passenger and freight service. She was an odd-looking craft, embodying in her build the lessons learned in the ice of early and late winter by her predecessors on the ferry route. Her hull had been built in Britain, sent out and put together on the St Lawrence: the hull was punt-shaped, with iron frames and side-plates, but planked with heavy elm under water. She had paddle engines; the wheels were heavily built for ice breaking. The ferry-boat waddled back and forth from Wolfe Island to the city half a dozen times a day, always calling at our island. In fine summer weather she took most extraordinary loads of freight on her bow-deck, which had the effect of lifting the stern and giving her a look as it were of a huge duck about to dive.

Only the day-to-day traffic between islands and town, farm produce in one direction and commodities equally commonplace in the other—yet in midstream you could see (and you can still see it to-day) Frontenac's vision of great waters. Ashore he saw only the forest: to-day you see the limestone buildings of Kingston to the North, the green shores beyond them to the West. Then there is a glimpse out over the open lake—you can go twelve hundred miles inland by lake and river that way. Next, the islands bound the view for half the circle; a break again and a peep for fifteen miles downstream—you can go out a thousand miles to the Atlantic that way. Follow the mainland back upstream: you see the old stone fort with the Union Jack over it—and perhaps the white puff of smoke from the "Noon gun"—the Martello towers, the ruins of the military hospital, Navy Bay, the Royal Military College, then the "causeway" with its bascule bridge over the Cataraqui River, to Kingston again.

The ferry-boat was a clearing-house for the gossips of the islands. On market days the ferry brought together many people who otherwise would have seen each other only at long intervals. There were political arguments, too. On the return trip from the city, rival partisans heated by the drinks that had accompanied their bargainings with cheese and cattle buyers sometimes came to blows—"Grit" against Tory or Orange against "Green".

At certain seasons one could see very special passengers on board—the Anglican or Roman Catholic archbishop going to

hold Confirmation or Mass on Wolfe Island, a former islander
who had "made money" in the United States, the owner-
driver of a touring stallion—his "great horse" securely tied
up on the bow-deck, the well-known American angler from
"down in Ohio" who came every summer to fish for black
bass, the city specialist called in consultation by the general
practitioner on Wolfe Island, a politician on his way to
address a meeting, the professor of Geology from the university
taking his students to see glacial scorings in the limestone. Of
all these the angler was by far the most interesting, the rod-
cases that lay with his luggage made a young fisherman almost
intolerably curious.

To cross the wide river "to town" on a lowering autumn
day of strong South West wind was a complete voyage for a
small boy who had been brought up among vessels. The
ferry-boat came in, put out her lines bow and stern, the gang-
plank was thrown out—though one jumped aboard rather
than use it. "Let go!" was heard from the wheelhouse, the
lines came in as the engine started, we were off. One went
along the alley-way past the engine-room and up to the
promenade deck; soon we were out from under the lee of the
island and began to feel wind and wave. Both increased as we
got out into midstream, the boat began to roll. At intervals
heavier seas struck and splashed aboard a bit, a man went out
on the bow-deck to secure a wagon that had begun to move,
but all too soon we were through it and were going ashore.
Little did the town people know, as we walked up Brock
Street and across the Market Square, what rough water we
"sailors" had just crossed!

Chapter VI

THE ICE

§ I. THE FREEZING OF THE LAKE

If the invention of the thermometer had preceded the discovery of the St Lawrence, would the white man have gone back to Europe? Did he stay only because he did not know how cold it really was? Be that as it may, extremes of cold (and heat) misrepresent the climate of eastern Canada. Remember the long temperate intervals, and above all the clear skies. The advertising of "hours of sunshine" in England never fails to give the Canadian a shock.

But about ice. Lake Ontario seldom freezes across its full width of fifty miles and, when it does, the wind breaks up the ice. All the bays and protected waters, however, freeze over; Kingston Harbour is a good example, from mid-January to early April it is frozen to a depth of ten to twenty inches. The ice "takes", as we say, differently in different years. Obviously it must begin when cold and calm coincide; sometimes the first thin film thickens undisturbed during three or four cold still days and becomes "the ice" of that year. Sometimes the wind breaks it up once or twice before it "takes" for the winter. The thin broken ice may disappear down the river or out on to the lake, or it may be blown against a lee-shore and freeze into a mass, hundreds of acres of it, like jumbled broken glass, leaving only part of the harbour to freeze over smoothly.

Many years ago I skated, with a younger brother, across Kingston Harbour to Garden Island (two miles) on new ice, perhaps two inches thick, just as it was beginning to crack up in a strong South wind. At first the waves break only the far-off edges of the new ice; then with a fifty mile sweep behind it the wave-form gets under the ice and begins to crack it more and more. When it has got into its full stride—well, it is better not to be out on the ice. However, we had started without realizing how far this cracking process had gone. We began to notice the water rising through the cracks as we crossed them, the only thing was to keep going as fast as we could. A loosened bootlace was a complication, for it meant stopping—we had to watch for a minute or two until we were on a big enough uncracked area to stop safely. When we reached the island, after twenty minutes' skating, we found that we had been watched through glasses and that men had been ready to start out with the "ice-boat"—that craft is described elsewhere—if we had got into trouble. And we well might have, for three hours later the ice had broken up.

About four inches of ice will carry a horse. The first ones driven across were small and ancient animals, of no great value. A noose of stout rope was put round the horse's neck on these early trips, the end of it handy in the sleigh. If the horse went through, the thing to do was to jump out on the ice, let go the traces, run along in front of the horse and haul him out. It is said that a horse can help himself a good deal, in getting up on the ice again; but I cannot describe this rather exciting business, for I have never seen a horse go through the ice, either the early ice or the failing ice in the spring—the firm's chief teamster used to ask me to go along with him "for luck"! This man and I have stood in the box-sleigh, he driving and I with the rope ready in my hands, and crossed very unsafe ice without accident, though the horse might often put a foot through. But that is not to say that accidents were specially rare; horses were lost through the ice every year, most often by farmers who used the ice only occasionally. We had one horse that had been got out, exhausted, after a long time in the icy water—he shied at the smallest puddle ever afterwards.

The length of time needed to pass from these precarious conditions to what was called "good crossing"—ten to sixteen inches of ice—varied according to two factors, snow and temperature. Snow is an almost perfect insulator (think of the Arctic "igloo"), a few inches of snow lying evenly over new ice will prevent even "below zero" from thickening it. Conversely, if no snow falls on the new ice it will thicken rapidly without any extreme cold. As soon as the ice was "safe", roads were marked out by evergreen branches set at short intervals. Similar lines of "Christmas trees" surrounded the areas where the ice was being cut. The expansion and contraction of the mature ice always produced one or two cracks, which winter by winter were usually in the same places. These cracks were not open seams but rather, as it were, folds in the ice; sometimes heaved up, sometimes almost level. Occasionally they were real barriers, one had to search for a place to get across. The crack that ran from the Kingston waterfront to Cedar Island had a stout bridge of planks built over it where the road crossed it, so that heavy loads would not crack the edges of the ice as they passed over.

Up to about thirty-five years ago, "the ice" on Kingston Harbour served many purposes, it saw varied activities. The gunners of the field artillery used to practise, long ago, with their smooth-bore guns, at a target set out on the ice a couple of miles South West of Fort Henry: the island boys of that time (they are very old men to-day) used to chase the heavy round shot as they rolled along the ice and take them home as trophies. The Canadian game of ice-hockey originated here. All skating and curling, before the day of covered rinks and of skating and curling clubs, was on "the ice". A very heavy snowfall would stop these activities completely, but willing hands cleared "rinks" after ordinary storms. The first ice is flinty hard and not perfectly smooth: there were times, however, usually in March after the first spring rains had melted the snow and smoothed the surface, and this surface had refrozen, when there were literally square miles of perfect ice for skating. Skate-sailing then came in, and good fun it was; a little triangular spritsail carried on the shoulder and leaned into against the wind-pressure, took one along at a good rate. Trotting races were sometimes held when the ice was right; the drivers in their short, high sleighs sat close up to the horse's hind-quarters as they do in their "sulkies" on the "dirt" trotting-tracks. All horses were "sharp-shod" for work on the ice, these trotters especially. When at full speed a spray of fine white particles of ice leaped up from their flying hooves. More prosaic was the annual cutting and hauling ashore of ice for summer use. At Garden Island, the schooners, as they lay frozen in for the winter, used often to be loaded with ice for delivery in the spring to American ports on Lake Erie. After heavy snowfalls there was some snow-shoeing, but it never became very popular. Ice-yachting was the favourite sport; there were races every year with American clubs from the New York State shores.

All these activities have gone. Speed was the thrill of ice-yachting, and the motor car has eclipsed it. Machine-made ice is cheaper than natural ice. Hockey is played in regulation rinks, under organized league schedules. In fact professional hockey is "Big Business", a money-making gladiatorial show; artificial ice made it independent of the weather, and has enabled it to spread all over the continent, and to Europe. And so on—the simpler ways have disappeared. The present generation knows nothing of "the ice" as it was used thirty-five years ago, when, in fair weather or foul, we crossed it every day—on foot, in glaring sunlight and still cold clear air; in wild snowstorms, when one had to follow the road and keep the next bush in sight; in the mild blowy days of March,

8-2

with cloud-shadows sliding over the snow; occasionally on snow-shoes, over deep new-fallen snow that covered ice and land without a break in the dazzling surface; at times on skates, when the ice was temptingly smooth; again, by sleigh, often comfortable in fur coat and under a fur "buffalo-robe", often sitting on top of a heavy load, the horses slogging along at a walk; sometimes through cold rain that drove in sheets before the wind; sometimes at night, the snow giving back the moonlight. Perhaps the pleasantest recollection, walking or driving, is of crossing while the red ball of the sun was sinking behind the level plain of ice and snow, and lights began to show in Kingston and on the islands—a lovely scene.

I have been told that in recent winters motor cars on the ice have become a common sight. I have not seen them, and do not want to see them. Is it too conservative, too reactionary, to feel that it is almost sacrilege so to use "the ice", like any common highway? Will the poster-advertiser follow the motor car? Heaven forbid!

§ 2. THE ICE-BOAT

Our little village of four hundred souls, on Garden Island, was not self-supporting. Communication with Kingston, for food, mails, the doctor and so on, had to be maintained. Sport, ice-cutting and heavy hauling went on only under favourable conditions; and, while the ice was "safe", the only discomforts in crossing it were on days of storm and severe cold. The difficulty was the "between seasons" crossing, when a steamer could not get through the ice, and the ice could not carry any load. There was often only a day or two of these conditions when the ice was forming, but they might last for a fortnight when the ice was going away in the spring. The sun breaks the ice up into an infinite number of fine vertical spikes or needles, whose length is the thickness of the ice, which becomes something like a vast honeycomb. The cold nights bind it together again and harden the surface; it takes many days to break down ice 18–20 inches thick, but the sun and rain finally soften it so that the wind or a steamer can break it up.

During the intervals between solid ice and open water the "ice-boat" was used. An odd craft, really a punt, lightly but strongly built of wood and sheathed with thin sheet metal.

Ice-boat

About 22 feet long, 4 feet 6 inches wide and 20 inches deep, flat-bottomed and square ended, it had steel-shod runners under it, which kept the boat about 5 inches off the ice. Ordinarily it was pushed along the ice by three or four men, wearing long rubber boots and short jackets. A spritsail on a short mast helped when possible; in open water both oars and sail were used. At each side of the square bow and stern were projecting hardwood handles, between which walked the leader and his second-in-command. Fixed in the gunwales, in pairs opposite one another, three or four on each side, were iron rods ending in rings like short bits of pipe. Through each pair of opposing rings was thrust a hardwood pole about $1\frac{1}{2}$ inches in diameter, and long enough to project about 2 feet beyond the boat on each side. These rods were about 3 feet above the ice, and each projecting end of each of them could be used, by a man walking on the ice, to shove the craft along. The "greenhorn" was put at a side-rod, and the first thing he had to learn was to walk close up to the rod, knocking his thighs against it at each step, and ready always to support his weight on it, on his stiffened arms, if the ice gave way under him. Otherwise he might go down to his waist, or even to his neck, in the icy water—to the great joy of the veterans in the crew. When one worked between the stern-handles, the "bobbing" action of the rest of the crew was a curious thing to see—the shove given with each step caused a sharp jerk of the shoulders through the stiffly held arms. And one's own action was exactly the same, of course!

Can you see this heavy punt, laden with perhaps six or eight hundredweight of goods, being hauled and shoved along by four or five men over the uncertain ice? All goes well for a time, nothing but physical force is needed. Suddenly the laden boat goes through the soft ice, the men's weight instantly added to it as they save themselves by sitting on the gunwales or the decked-in ends. Poles are got out, slowly the boat is pushed and coaxed along until the men at the bow reach firmer ice. The sloping "punt" bow helps them to haul the boat up on the ice again; perhaps only to go through the next moment. Back-breaking work, but more a matter of knack and skill, based upon knowledge of the job, than one of any great strength. Big heavy men were not good at it, as a rule.

Passengers were not popular in the ice-boat, least of all women. Great pains were taken to scare them; by causing the craft to take sudden and unnecessary lurches it might be possible to keep them from asking again to be taken "over to town". There was a story of one of the island lake-captains (not the one of whom there is a sketch elsewhere in this book) who refused to be a passenger. An expert ice-boat man himself, he had got drunk in town and headed home across the unsafe ice, alone. The ice-boat overtook him, and the crew tried to make him get aboard; but he wouldn't. He continued to evade them all the way across, and got safely ashore—he knew the unpopularity of human "dead-weight" in the ice-boat, and "wasn't having any".

One trip stands out vividly, perhaps the only one I ever made that was really risky, not to say dangerous. It was a warm day in mid-April, there was a thin fog over the cold black ice, rain and thunderstorms were not far off. As we left Kingston we found the ice in its most exasperating mood. It bent like rubber under the weight of ice-boat and men, but like rubber it did not break. The water rose through the sagging "honeycombed" ice, so that every inch of progress was uphill, so to speak, and with no prospect of getting to the top; the pool on the ice moved along with the boat. A quarter of a mile out, we met the ice-boat bringing the U.S. mails; the man in charge warned us to turn back, saying that it was "hell out there". That was all, but the man happened to be a former employee of our firm, who had left because of a row of some sort; so no suggestions from him. On we went. When we had struggled out for another half-mile (it was two miles, you remember, to our island), there came sheets of rain with a violent thunderstorm. Our boat was leaking a bit from the unusual strain, the addition of heavy rain meant that one man had to bail at short intervals. When we were about half-way across, the rain stopped, and it began to blow from the West. Presently it blew really hard, and one saw with unwilling eyes that the ice was moving—and speaking, too, in the most threatening of all its many voices. A low, menacing hiss came from the irregular lines of pushed-up "needles" that showed white against the sullen green-black surface of the ice, as its weak spots were found out by the pressure. One squeeze, if we were caught at such a spot, would have sunk the ice-boat; her square model made her a very bad subject for such a test. We turned down stream at once, before the wind, and set the sail to help us to keep moving. We broke through again and again, it was very hard work to keep going at all. After half an hour of this we seemed to clear the moving ice, or rather it had got jammed in the narrowing channel. We could then turn right again and make for our objective, the East end of Garden Island. We were very wet and tired and hungry, but the worst was over; we reached the island at the end of perhaps three hours, during which we had covered, including the detour, only about three and a half miles. And we landed just in time, for it soon blew a gale and by evening the harbour was clear for miles, with the broken-up ice jammed across the river in a grinding heaving line of white—about at the point where we had made our second turn, for the last lap of our trip.

Does middle-age exaggerate such a risk, looking back upon it? At any rate one remembers the veteran French-Canadian who was in charge of the ice-boat that day saying that he was "never so dam' glad t' get ashore, never!"

§ 3. FOR SAILORS ONLY

Ice-yachts of various forms have been built and sailed in widely separated parts of the northern world, wherever favourable conditions occurred. Before the petrol engine changed our ideas of speed by land and air, the speed of the ice-yacht had a unique attraction. It was the highest speed ever made under wind-power, as ice-hockey is the fastest game played under bodily power only.

The necessary conditions for ice-yachting—heavy smooth ice on lakes and wide rivers, combined with a not too severe winter, in which frequent thaws keep the ice reasonably clear of snow—are fairly general in north-eastern North America, where the ice-yacht attained its highest development. The American ice-yachtsman brought the craft to the point of dependable performance; the fastest yachts on

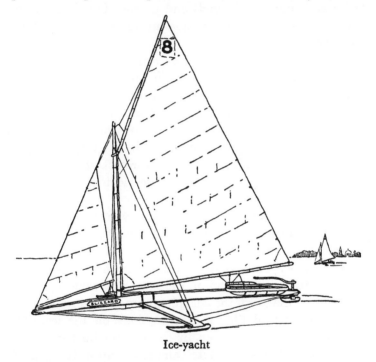

Ice-yacht

Kingston Harbour were of a type first developed on the Hudson River above New York. Their form, at the peak of the popularity of ice-yachting about 1900, had the simplicity that always goes with correct design. Perhaps by referring to the illustration the reader can follow a short description of their build and rig.

They were built, preferably from basswood for lightness, of two members only—one lengthwise about 30–40 feet long resting on and fastened to a cross-plank of about 16–24 feet spread, set about 12–16 feet from the "bow". Wire-rope stays, tightened by turnbuckles, joined the ends of the cross-plank and the lengthwise member; the mast (which always raked forward, not aft) was set 2–3 feet forward of the cross-plank and stayed to its ends and to the "bow". A strong wire-rope bobstay ran fore-and-aft under the lengthwise member.

The yacht sailed on three skates, one under each end of the cross-plank and a smaller one aft, the rudder-skate. All three were of oak, shod with polished cast-iron cut to a **V**-edge where it rested on the ice. Right aft was a little cushioned cockpit about 8 feet long in which two could lie down, one on each side of the main length-piece of wood. The long tiller (5–6 feet) came over one's hip as he lay in the cockpit: the sheets of mainsail and staysail were brought to cleats fastened to the main length-piece, close at hand.

From 300 to 500 square feet of very light canvas were carried in mainsail and staysail. The aim of the designer was to bring the combined "centre of effort" of the sails exactly over the cross-plank, that is to say over the skates as they took the drive of the wind on the sails. The whole craft was so balanced that with the cockpit empty, a man standing on the "bow" would lift the steering-skate off the ice. The weight of one or two men in the cockpit held down the steering-skate to make it "bite" and give control at high speed.

The yachts, naturally, bore wintry names—"Jack Frost", "Snow Bird", "North Wind", "Blizzard". And one had to wear wintry kit when sailing them, for even in mild weather there were wind and speed to be reckoned with. The usual outfit was a fur cap down over ears and forehead, and a long coonskin coat (fifty dollars bought a good one in those days, as against three hundred dollars to-day). A bit of rope or a strip of canvas tied tightly round the waist outside the coat was an added warmth, it kept the wind from getting up inside! Trousers were tucked into high overshoes fitted with "creepers" for gripping the ice: loose mittens, never gloves, were worn. Oddly enough, no goggles were used; perhaps they came in with the motor age?

Picture a fine afternoon in March after a day or two of thaw, the rain has washed the ice clear of snow. There have been perhaps eight or ten degrees of frost over night; fourteen square miles of ice as smooth as ice can be are waiting to be enjoyed in a brisk twelve-mile breeze from the West. In such conditions it was a delight to handle one of these odd craft, curiously different from sailing afloat. The chief difference was that an ice-yacht travels much faster than the wind that drives it, thirty to forty miles an hour in moderate winds was quite usual. And one got the full "feel" of the speed, in the open rush of air, close down to the ice which streamed back under the craft as it rushed smoothly along—it was "the poetry of motion".

Another obvious difference from sailing afloat was the ability to stop where and when one liked by simply pointing the yacht up into the wind. The craft carried way for some distance, on smooth ice; the usual thing was to sit up in the cockpit and drag the pointed "creepers" on one's overshoes along the ice, to check the speed. Ice-yachts sailed incredibly close to the wind; the distance they would "reach", when going about, was always an astonishment, at first, to the water sailor. They sailed fastest with the wind abeam and with sheets hauled "flat aft". Before the wind they were useless, because the friction between skates and ice was so slight that they slid away from the wind and lost their speed, then surged violently forward (with a strong tendency to swing off their course) when the unbalanced mainsail filled again.

The usual racing distance for the ice-yachts was 12 miles, three times round a triangular course. A good deal of nonsense was talked about the terrific speeds attained in these races, but fast time was made, nevertheless. It was quite common for all the yachts in a race to finish well under the half-hour, occasionally the winner's time might be 21–22 minutes. Since the distance covered in making the three rounds would be 18–20 miles, this means averaging about 55 miles an hour. The fastest I have ever seen (and I am quite sure I have never sailed so fast myself!) was 1¾ miles in 1½ minutes, or 70 miles an hour. The man who did it told me afterwards that his craft was only just under control on that leg of the course!

All things considered, there were very few accidents. In races some wild chances were taken, and conditions were not always ideal, whether on race days or in the ordinary run of sailing. For example, it was not pleasant, at high speed, to have a skate drop into a crack—nor was it very good for the fabric of the ice-yacht. Occasionally the ice was covered with thin flat patches of drifted snow; one could plough right through them—if he carried enough sail! Once, on a day like this, my windward skate ran into a patch of snow which was much deeper than it had appeared to be. Instantly the yacht, which was of an old type with too much sail aft, whipped up into the wind and stopped with a violent jerk. I found myself out in the bank of snow at full length, eyes and mouth full of snow and with snow up my sleeves and down my neck. A second later I found I still held the tiller, which pointed straight out over the stern of the yacht. My passenger was picking himself up out of another snowbank twenty yards away. I remember wondering how he had missed hitting the cross-plank as he shot out of the cockpit. "That'll do, take me home", he said, laughing dubiously as he came back to help get the yacht out of the snow.

There was always an interest in sailing under unusual and unsuitable conditions. For instance there were times when on smooth ice in a gale of wind one could sail at fair speed "under bare poles", and the merest rag of canvas drove the yacht along like a thing possessed. Or, if there was wind enough, one might sail when the surface of the ice, for two or three inches deep, had been softened by the spring sun. Carrying full sail, in a strong breeze that on hard smooth ice would have meant reefing down, one tore happily along, leaving deep tracks in the soft surface. The trick in this sailing was to keep moving, especially not to lose way when "going about". Some ice-yachtsmen liked to sail when there was rainwater, perhaps an inch or two of it, lying on the ice. The effect of the water was the same as the soft surface, one carried more sail to overcome its drag on the yacht's skates. It was wise to wear an oilskin coat for this business, in case of hitting pools of deeper water—it splashed!

Whatever the conditions, "putting up" the yacht after a sail was always the same routine. One came close inshore, stopped, lowered and stowed the sails. The staysail was often detachable, and went into the cockpit—otherwise it had its own cover. The newer-type craft had a big sail-cover that laced in front of the mast and covered in the stowed sails and the cockpit. When all was snug, the craft was lifted up on to three stout trestles, or heavy wood blocks, one just inside each of the three skates. The tiller was always taken ashore, for obvious reasons—as one threw it over his shoulder he looked once more to see that everything was as it should be—what a long time ago it all seems!

Chapter VII

QUEEN'S

§ 1. THE FOUNDATION

A generation had passed after the coming of the Loyalists to Upper Canada before the University movement effectually began. In the Maritime Provinces it started earlier; for there (according to the common story) the settlers were mainly from New England where letters and culture had been for a century and a half on a higher level than in the other colonies. Thus we are proudly told by the men of King's College, Halifax, that theirs is the oldest university of British America (founded at Windsor, 1788). It was not till the period of George IV and William IV that in Upper Canada the demand for university education reached any fulfilment. Even then, when the charters for the foundation of colleges were obtained, the acquisition of funds and of buildings, the engagement of teachers and the assembling of classes, were slower matters and of more labour. It was one thing to secure the charter, another to open the college.

The first beginning is associated with Toronto. A young Presbyterian had come from Scotland—it is noticeable how many Canadian universities have Scottish names or at least Scotsmen among their founders; this young man became first an Anglican, and later a bishop, the most famous bishop of English-speaking Canada, and perhaps as really significant as Archbishop Laval the Frenchman of earlier days; and he played a leading part in the foundation of King's College, Toronto. The repetition of the title will not escape notice; Canada was, as it still is, the King's country. Strachan was determined that the college should be, as Oxford and

Cambridge still were, a private preserve of the Church of England. But it is on record that the settlers of Ontario and the Scots who followed them were generally not Anglican; Richard Cartwright at the time said nineteen-twentieths of them were not; and among those excluded by Strachan there arose a natural desire to have a college or colleges of their own, with their own charters. The Methodists tell us that their Victoria College at Cobourg was the first non-Anglican foundation to be opened outside Scotland; but long ago they moved it to Toronto, content that it should become a constituent college, along with what had been King's and is now University College, in the remodelled University of Toronto.

Queen's College was a Scottish and Presbyterian foundation; and there were those (we are told) who thought in 1839 of so naming it, the Scottish Presbyterian College. But the longer-headed prevailed; they obtained a charter from Queen Victoria (16 October 1841); they decided that the classes should be open to students without religious tests; and teaching began in 1842 (7 March).

Roughly speaking, Queen's, McGill and Toronto all started about the same time (McGill twenty years ahead), as a result of a general feeling in the English-speaking community, very much as later on in England the so-called provincial Universities came into being within one generation in response to a similar sense that the highest range in education should be readily available. The population in Canada in the 'thirties was far smaller than in England in the 'nineties, but the distances were greater. Leeds and Sheffield, Liverpool and Manchester are not 160 miles apart as the three Canadian universities are. Road and river were the only means of communication, and when about 1830 Sir George Head drove in his sleigh from Montreal to Kingston it took him five days. The earliest Canadian railway ran its first train in 1836 over some 16 miles in another part of the country. To-day a good train does Sir George's journey in 3½ hours.

The history of a university or a college is commonly rather monotonous; there is a family likeness about one and another, and the early days of all of them are almost painfully alike. In the Middle Ages, of course, a university was often *not* founded; it occurred, it grew, it migrated, and in course of time it organized itself, developed "nations" or colleges, and migrated no more. So far as it was "founded" at all, students and professors made it for themselves. In more modern times princes and states, provinces and plutocrats, have founded universities; the city of Edinburgh led the way in this among our peoples after the Reformation. It is obvious that, where an organized community, with the power of levying taxes (and actually getting them paid), or a super-millionaire, as at Leland Stanford, does the founding, the story is vastly different. Queen's belongs to neither of these categories; like a score of other colleges in the United States and elsewhere, it was the creation of enthusiasts, often with more ideas than dollars—perhaps as much a dream and an ideal as a creation; but, as with many other colleges, the dream was fulfilled, the dream became a reality, a struggling reality, an organism battling for life, with a precarious hold on life; and then the dangerous period of infancy was passed, life was assured, and other risks and perils followed. Development means transformation, triumph and disappointment, change; and what we dreamed becomes something we never thought of; like our other children this child of our dreams grows up, takes its own way with an independence that seems natural in ourselves and our contemporaries but somehow not quite so natural in those we have nurtured.

It is not our task here to tell of the first fifty years of Queen's—that oft-told tale of high hopes, brave men and no funds, too familiar to those who know the universities of the

New World. The difficulties were immense in any case; and then the college had hardly opened its doors—and lowly doors they were, in a small frame house, on the north side of Colborne Street in Kingston—when the Disruption came in Scotland, and a parallel movement in Canada brought fresh disunion among Presbyterians, and darkened the college future from the start. The staff were such as could be found; there was little or nothing to tempt men of the first rank of scholarship to this or any other new-born college; but Queen's had men who at any rate loved learning. The first Principal of the united University of Aberdeen, Dr Campbell, had been Professor of Classics in Queen's; and Queen's gave Aberdeen yet another Principal, eighty or more years later, in Hamilton Fyfe. Somehow or other—*superanda omnis fortuna ferendo est*—the college hung together; even the blackest of black years 1868-9 did not wreck it, nor the withdrawal of Provincial Government aid, when the Queen's people were so wicked as to prefer to go on existing somehow by themselves "on the old Ontario strand" and not become another nice little college, swallowed up in a huge city, a mere constituent part of the "provincial" university. It was a brave decision, and time has proved it a wise one. There are few things so disastrous in a nation's education as to have it all of one type, and that type devised by a government anxious as to the voting of a democracy. Standardization is our prime danger to-day—one board of education "guiding" all our schools, one B.B.C. controlling our music, our thoughts, our pronunciation, one "Book of the Month Club" closing the last door to independence of mind.

The struggle made Queen's, as a like struggle on a larger scale made Scotland. Would it not have been better, easier, financially more expedient and so forth, to have incorporated Queen's in the provincial university, Scotland in England? Edward I thought so, and possibly others; but the world has gained by Scotland's struggle for survival, as Scotland gained herself, for it made the Scots; and we need not pause here to speak of them as empire-builders and world-makers. Their names are written on our rivers; are not Mackenzie and Fraser, rivers of Canada—but we need not paraphrase Naaman. Queen's was from the start pre-eminently Scottish, modelled on Edinburgh, founded, taught and believed-in by Scots, a monument of Scottish character, a stronghold of Scottish religion; and it would not be sunk in a government institution. It meant struggle and poverty—

Yet still the blood is strong, the heart is Highland—

and it meant an independent type, a challenge, a contrast, the something different that keeps thought alive.

§ 2. THE COLLEGE WE KNEW

It was perhaps expected that Queen's College would be at the Capital of the Government. But when Confederation came, either because there were too many Orangemen at the old Loyalist centre, or because (as Goldwin Smith suggested) "the lumber village nearest the North Pole" seemed safer from the Americans, or because an entirely new town, without a legend, on a fine site, between French and English provinces, appeared best, Kingston did not become the Capital of the Dominion, nor yet of the Province. It was to remain a small town with a history and a university. Whoever may regret the decisions that selected the two capitals, the university at least has no cause to deplore them. There may be much to be said for having a university in a great town like London or Berlin; there is surely as much for having it in a quieter and friendlier, like Heidelberg, or like Oxford in the days before the motor-car industry turned it (as some humourist has said) into the "Quartier Latin" of Cowley. Has Yale, for instance, gained from having 40,000 Italians at its

door, or Harvard from the Irish city council of a swollen
Cambridge? Kingston keeps, as was said by the Principal of a
Scottish university forty years ago, a dignity of its own—in
spite of feverish efforts made at times by its town council to
make it commonplace. But that is perhaps to be expected of
town councils and mayors; did not Andrew Lang indignantly
complain that Provost Playfair had found St Andrews
picturesque and left it sanitary? So there Queen's stands—in
a small town on the lake, a town with a history, as we have
seen, a town of many charms. It is not that the capitals
moved away from her; she decided, as we have seen, not to
move after them. As the students' song definitely says:

> On the old Ontario strand, my boys,
> Where Queen's for evermore shall stand,
> For has she not stood
> Since the time of the flood,
> On the old Ontario strand?

In 1872 a new professor came from Scotland. He took a
cab at the station, and watched the town as he drove through.
He reached at last a noble building with a dome; "then the
college has some good buildings", he said to himself; but the
cab drove on—past the Courthouse—and John Watson found
himself on a campus of some size with two buildings—a fine
old country house with two wings, well set above its surround-
ings, and a conscientious structure behind it. The latter by
1896 was the Medical School; and of it, on the addition of a
third storey, Principal Grant is said to have remarked that the
architect had achieved the impossible; he had made the
ugliest building in the world uglier. But the days were to
come when higher standards in ugliness, at Queen's, and in
many other places, should be reached, and the Medical
Building, deprived after a fire of its top storey, should look
reasonable again.

But Grant came in 1877 and saw at once that more

accommodation was needed, and achieved it. The old Arts building, with its tower and the library in the rounded end, rose. In 1880, the Princess Louise, with her husband, the Marquis of Lorne, then Governor-General, laid the foundation stone. Some extra expenditure was proposed in honour of the occasion; they were times when every dollar counted; but Principal Grant was ready with the homely proverb of the village, apt if odd in this connection: "We don't kill a pig every day." The tower may be rather too small for the size of the building, yet the aspect, especially since the trees of the campus have grown, is a pleasing one. For some time the building was sufficient; and then the Carruthers Hall was erected for Applied Sciences. In 1896 a lowlier effort was added behind it, a chaste frame building, something in the style of Noah's Ark, to be an engineering laboratory. It did not please the students so much as its builder, who proudly said it might well be cased in brick. This was never done, but one morning the university and the town found painted on the wooden walls in huge letters TOOL HOUSE. Paint and brushes and overalls had been bought in some other town; and they were carefully burnt after the completion of the inscription. It was never discovered who did the job, but it was well known unofficially. The inscription was duly painted over, but it remained legible for decades; and one of the miscreants (a happy lad he was) lived to have an honorary degree from Queen's.

This then was the extent of the university buildings in 1896—all within the big campus that seemed painfully ragged and unkempt to a British eye familiar with the academic lawns of England. Next year came Andrew Drummond, and told the trustees that this must not be; they must allow him funds to tidy the place; and with their permission he started with fifty dollars. It is another scene now, and long has been.

Plate XI

Old Arts Building, Queen's

Yes, to an Old Country eye there was a roughness, something unfinished, about the whole aspect of the place, in striking contrast with the graceful buildings of Trinity College, Toronto, the second creation of Bishop Strachan when Fate and the Government took King's College under their care and he (in Goldwin Smith's phrase) started off in a cockboat of his own. But a Classical scholar should have remembered how in Aeschylus' play it is written that not walls but men make the city; and in time he realized it. Grant brought his newcomer into a very remarkable body of men. How exactly they had been recruited, it would be difficult now to recall. One man was a minister whose throat had gone wrong, but who had a wide knowledge (of the old kind) of Field Botany, and knew and loved the flowers of Canada. Another was sent by Edward Caird—recommendation enough. Yet another came on a clergyman's assurance that he was good at his Classics—an appointment that might well have turned out very wrong, and was amazingly right.

The fact is that professors can be too wisely and too efficiently selected; and Queen's, by good luck or good management, had escaped two of the chief perils in selecting a staff. There is the danger of the "home-made", "one of our own men"—an obvious way of being loyal to your own, but, as many colleges have found—or, at least, others have noticed it in them—it is a reliable way to become second-rate; and Grant had "no belief in second-rate universities". Let tact excuse our not mentioning instances, but there are great societies, quite easy to name, that have suffered for too great loyalty to "our own men". There is again the type that Sainte-Beuve somewhere calls the "bon élève"—the "good student" as we used to name them at Queen's. Every lesson learnt, every examination passed, every possible distinction acquired, a perfect record on paper—and that is all; "a tank", as our trustee from Caithness called a man of the kind; "an echo and not a voice", was another description. But sometimes they do not even echo.

We were happier. Our buildings were overcrowded, our campus ragged, our equipment meagre (one lantern and one telephone for the lot of us)—but we had men, voices not echoes, and voices that stirred the dead or the unborn, whichever you prefer to call them. Of course, we suffered from examination products—we had one or two on the staff, downright "bons élèves"—and a good few in the classrooms; but Queen's bred men in those days. If we did not make scholars or great researchers in Science, we gave Canada men, and men who have served her well. It was John Watson's conception of a University that dominated us, a society whose function was "to break up men's dogmatism and set them at a universal point of view". Plato was before him there, in wishing his ideal man to be "spectator of all time and all existence"; but, unlike Greek philosophers in general, we were a society. Something may be done by methods in education; ideas are more potent; but as the Highland woman said: "We owe everything to people."

A happy society it was in the main—of men, mostly married, who could therefore see one another when they chose and keep away if they preferred. Our incomes were much on a level, and our tastes and subjects differed; there was a certain amount of quiet entertainment—perhaps a little dull now and then, but we liked one another, and that covers a good deal of dullness; we had an essay society the "Saturday Club", college business, our own hobbies, books and interests. There was a suitable amount of passing squabble and gentle scandal to keep life bright, without making tempers too edgy; we could disagree sharply enough, perhaps quarrel a little at times, and yet recognize the good qualities of the other man, forget his sharp words (and one's own) and be good friends again. But why elaborate? It was

essentially a college society. We were, of course, a University
and could give degrees—of course, of course! But a University nowadays is one thing and a college another. We
were both.

Here a slight digression may be forgiven, for "University"
has different meanings in England, Scotland and America.
The stranger in Cambridge asks where the university is; and
it is nowhere. In Cambridge, as in Oxford, the university is
a society, not a building or series of buildings. Nor is the
wholly modern American distinction between a college
where some subjects are taught and a university where all
may be studied, founded on the Latin language, on medieval
usage or on British tradition; it seems to rest on a false conception of the meaning of *universitas*, even if modern Greeks
have adopted it in their *panepistemion*. A further point
deserves notice; besides being in itself a university (a degree-
giving body) Queen's College differed from the colleges of
somewhat similar name in Oxford and Cambridge in that it
was not a self-governing society. A body of trustees was over
all, but wisely left all that concerned teaching and examination, degrees and research, to the Professors in session as the
"Senate". More significant was the Principal, standing
somewhere between the beneficent controller of the Scottish
university and the absolute despot of the American. Grant
was trained in Scotland, and the Queen's tradition was
Scottish; so the lot of the professor was very tolerable, tem-
pered by friendship and sense; it might have been very
different.

A genial and friendly body our Senate was. There was
J. B. Mowat, one of the earliest students that Queen's
enrolled, our Hebraist, but, as a college song suggested, not
quite a modernist—

Does you know the gentle Rabbi who makes the critics quail?
Does you know that he can demonstrate that Jonah ate the whale?

Mowat was the brother of a Prime Minister, but "the gentle Rabbi" describes him, a kindly old man, who would sit meditatively at our discussions, and, if later on he owned that he had "had his doubts about it at the time", he never troubled us by telling them. There was Donald Ross, well-groomed and stately, but shy and a little silent—"a few cheering monosyllables" was a wicked colleague's summary of his talk. There was George D. Ferguson, with the Duke-of-Wellington nose that won him the nickname of "the Beak", who "lectured to us on the Middle Ages—from personal reminiscence". There was Archie Knight, once a headmaster, now Professor of Physiology, an expert in questions of fish-culture, ever the kindest and most congenial of companions, a man of generous temper and a smile that made and kept friends. There was Davie Marshall—"Pheesics" the boys called him—whose Physics may have been elementary (much that we did had to be): but he and his wife welcomed colleague and pupil to a great house, adorned with Japanese curiosities acquired by themselves in Japan and an ancient piano. It was the one house which even hinted at the collector's instinct or the art of the Orient; and there was good fare, followed by family prayers and Scottish song. Did he not once translate a song line by line for the benefit of an ignorant Sassenach?

> Duncan Grey cam' here to woo—
> Duncan Grey *came* [with great emphasis] here to couRt—
> [with a great rolling R]
> Ha! ha! the wooing o't!
> Ha! ha! the couRting oFF it!

There was brave "Little Nicky"—Nicholson officially, who had resided on "the Pacific slope" and loved a resounding phrase. How could he throw that brawny ruffian downstairs as he had threatened to do, if the man didn't attend to what was going on? Nicholson was diminutive but undismayed: "He had the size", he said, "but I had the science!" Later on he assured a class that he *had* thrown him downstairs, and that he had died shortly after! Life did not dismay him, though most men would have shuddered at his life and circumstances. A victorious Nicky he was; and when a Scotsman came and gave us a lecture on Greek art and showed us the temple of the Wingless Nike, giving it a Scots-modern-Greek pronunciation, we all applauded. There was G. Y. Chown, our Registrar, efficient beyond our academic dreams, and kindliest of souls, but quite definite that fees must be paid. Hence the disturbance, when Grant's successor spoke of "that greatest danger to society—the educated criminal", and a student, whose views on finance may have been looser than Chown's, called out "That's you, G.Y.!" It was only after his death that it was discovered how many of these students he had himself helped to pay the fees that in his official capacity he so firmly demanded.

But outstanding above us all were four men—Nathan Dupuis, now long dead, an amazing mathematician, inventor of miraculous clocks, most precise of examiners (no budging *him* to lift a student four marks in Pass Mathematics, however brilliant the lad was elsewhere), a man incapable of compliment, but true and loyal; John Watson, philosopher, James Cappon, in English, (both of these from Glasgow), and the electric John Macnaughton from Aberdeen—and such colleagues no man has had. To have known them is

Part of our life's unalterable good.

Education—the very word has by now a dismal sound, a mere synonym for matriculation; and governments will establish "boards" to "administer" education, forgetful that the first board of education (*lignum scientiae* is the Latin; you will find it in the second chapter of Genesis) brought death into the world and all our woes. Carlyle is surely right, when,

in speaking of the use of a great book, he suggests that the real
education is to associate with a great man, a living man, to
watch his habits of mind, to share his interests, till you learn
not *what* he thinks (though you will learn that) but *how* he
thinks. This it was that some of the staff of Queen's gave us;
we lived with them and caught something of their way of
looking at things, learnt from them what the Greeks learnt
long before, that the fact is less important than the cause, that
it is the imponderables that count, that there is more beyond,
that the real life—the happy life—is that described by Fra
Lippo in Browning's poem:

> You've seen the world,
> The beauty and the wonder and the power,
> The shapes of things, their colours, lights and shades,
> Changes, surprises—and God made it all.

Looking back over forty years one feels that something of this
passed into every real Queen's man—something of it, at any
rate, and that these men bred this spirit. They opened our
eyes and gave us vision, they opened our minds and we began
to think.

§ 3. "JOHN"

"John" belongs to Queen's, let there be no doubt on that
score. Stephen Leacock said at a banquet in "John's"
honour, after a jocular review of his varied appointments at
Queen's, McGill and Toronto, "Long may he live to circu-
late among the Universities of Canada"; but, wherever he
went, Queen's remained his spiritual home, and his peers were
Grant, Watson, Shortt, Cappon and the rest of that great
group.

Let Queen's men think back to the old Convocation Hall,
thirty years ago—can you not see "John" leaning perilously
from the platform, striking a hand with a closed fist and
crying at the end of his argument: "Anyone with the eye of a

boiled codfish could see what I mean"—as indeed anyone should, it had been made so clear!

It was in talk, however, as one walked with him, or around the fire on a winter evening, that the essential quality of his utterance was best felt, when one found oneself straining to follow the allusions (and the adjectives!), at the same time wondering if he really would singe his fingers this time as one match after another burned down, or blew out as it was waved, without getting near the pipe. How he followed his listener, edging along the seat or standing closer and closer over him as the ideas developed, found expression, and opened up fresh side-issues! Was not one of Johnson's listeners "drowned" by the Doctor's talk? But he would revive, and go back for more, if he had any sense at all, as one went back and back again to "John's" fireside.

No man is perfect—both Johnson and "John" had their prejudices. One they had in common, and often most amusingly—Americans. Boswell relates that Dr Campbell quoted Johnson to him as having said of the Americans in 1769: "Sir, they...ought to be grateful for anything we allow them short of hanging." Impatient with American slowness in getting men to France in 1917, "John" burst out: "But what can be expected of a people whose leaders have names like Josephus, Tumulty and Macadoodledoo?" Nor did Canadian affairs during the War always meet with his approval. I asked him in his library in Montreal, one evening early in 1918, whether the story were true that he had said in an address after the 1917 "Conscription" election that everyone who voted for Laurier was a cockroach. "No, no," said he, "I was misreported in the newspapers. I did *not* say that everyone who voted for Laurier was a cockroach, but I *did* say that the cockroaches came out from behind the wainscots of Canada's kitchens to vote for him, and that's true!" Prohibi_ tion, in both Canada and the United States, always excited his scorn. "All that the Americans had given the world in art and culture could be wiped out and the world would be little the poorer; but they had achieved two great lagers, Schlitz at Milwaukee and Budweiser at St Louis; both had been thrown away." He was very fond of drawing a word-picture of the Goddess of Prohibition: "Aunt Jane, in a clean pinafore—a bottle of grape-juice in her left hand and a loving-cup of international soothing-syrup in her right." Of another aspect of our modern life, the chronic motor-traffic problem, he said: "The trouble is that too often there is forty horsepower under the bonnet and one asspower at the wheel."

In a letter from England a few years ago he wrote that the misuse of the dole was "rapidly turning the old mother of heroes into an incubator of paupers—suckers of the dole milk-bottle in proletarian perambulators".

Many outbursts were about literary things. He stood over me one evening just after the University of Toronto War Memorial had been dedicated, and demanded whether I had seen it. I had. "And what is cut on the cloister walls beside the roll of names?" "In Flanders fields the...." "No, no, I mean at the opposite end." "Nothing is here for tears, nothing to wail or knock the breast...." "Yes," he said, "and where is that from?" I silently thanked my lucky star that I knew, and said, "Milton's *Samson Agonistes*." "*Of course*," he burst out, "a Queen's man would know! Will you believe that I heard to-day a man not unknown in this University saying that he was not sure whether it was Shakespeare. His companion *knew* it was Shakespeare, but wasn't sure it was from *Lear*. Good Lord! not only not to know that it wasn't Shakespeare, but not to know that Milton was the *only* man who *ever* lived who had a mouth so shaped that out of it could come those words!"

Speaking of a well-known novelist's excursions into religious things: "It won't do," said "John", "he is like a

monkey that has strayed into a cathedral—instinct will make
him climb the nearest pillar, but, mark you, the higher he
climbs the more he exposes to view the less personable parts
of his anatomy." Dumas' *Three Musketeers* he characterized
as "the universal romantic heroes, not just national heroes",
and from this deduced their appeal to the youth of the world.
I cannot recall what Scottish ballad it was that he used to
quote to offset the effect produced upon him by the English
"Early one morning" with its refrain, "How could you use
a poor maiden so?" but I remember that he called the latter
"Boiled rabbit!" in a loud tone of scorn.

Of course the classics, especially his beloved Greeks, came
into his talk very often and in all sorts of ways. Stopping
before an engraving of Luke Fildes' Tate Gallery picture,
"The Doctor", he said: "The Greeks would not have
perpetuated such a moment of strain—compare that with
Myron's 'Discobolus', who is shown as just set to throw the
discus, not in the actual strain of throwing it." To illustrate
how much of New Testament thought is Greek, he quoted
St Paul: "the things which are seen are temporal, but the
things which are not seen are eternal", adding, with emphasis,
"That is Greek, no Hebrew ever had such a thought." No
teacher ever inspired the right sort of student more than
"John", but he was very impatient of the wrong sort—
"Mudturtles, flat-fish; Neptune with his trident couldn't get
them off the bottom!" To an honours student who made a
schoolboy's error in a prose exercise, he said: "Boys who did
that in Scotland died young—yes, and *unregretted.*"

Many comments on individuals remain in memory and
rumour—some of them have come to me from other listeners
to "John". Of a Scottish preacher, whom he had been recommended to hear, he said: "Nice young fellow, does his
best, but he's just a kitten...you can see the milk on his
whiskers." A very fine-looking divine of rather smooth and

unctuous ways he described as "an alabaster box of soft-soap". A very distinguished but also very untidy and uncouth Welshman, visiting Canada, he described as a "lousy old Merlin; fly-blown wizard", surely an apt union of blame and praise. One divine, not unknown in Canada in his day, he spoke of as "The stupidest man of my acquaintance —and I know what I am talking about, for I have a *very* large acquaintance of *very stupid people*!" Another man he credited with "a stupidity which surpasses nature and is contrary to it". Of a Canadian professor, "His mind is a muskeg of mediocrity", and of another, "going about clad in triple brass— no, in triple *blubber*, which is a deal harder to get through".

Of certain modern evangelists he said that they were "an example of a combination of modern business methods with (shall I say?) palaeolithic modes of thought". From a Kingston pulpit: "You were never meant to sit in a corner hatching the addled egg of your personal salvation." From another pulpit, speaking of the conventional idea of Heaven, he burst out, "Just imagine David Livingstone and men of his stamp sitting on golden chairs in a meadow of asphodel! In twenty-four hours they would be yawning their heads off, and in three days they would be turning the place into the Valhalla of their ancestors—what you might call a spiritual Donnybrook Fair."

"John" was a sincere admirer of Principal Grant. All Queen's men know in a general way of "Geordie's" achievements, but the older generation knew better what sacrifices he made and asked in her service. Without abating in the least his admiration for him, "John" liked to tell of the Principal's attempts to bring his staff also to make sacrifices. For instance, an outsider was usually brought in to give the special lectures at the Theological Alumni Conference, so once when "John" was to give them, Grant tried for Queen's sake to cut down the fee, because a lecturer living in Kingston had no travelling expenses to take out of it. Again, when the Principal had to make an important public appearance he would talk things over with his staff, separately and seriously. Later, listening to the Principal's address, one man after another might hear his ideas or suggestions being forcefully used in the cause of Queen's. "Any acknowledgment?" said "John", "none at all; when it was for Queen's the old Principal had a perfect virtuosity of predatoriness."

Carlyle speaks of men who are "the guides of the dull host...superior natures, whose eye is not destitute of free vision nor their heart of free volition". Of this select band all Queen's men who knew him will name "John" a member, crediting him perhaps most with that "free vision", that power to see through externals to essentials, which gave such tang to his criticisms, denunciations and eulogies, but also with that "free volition", that power to make his own judgment and to give it striking expression. It was not surprising to hear him say on one occasion: "I cannot remember ever having been bored." Was it not R.L.S., one of "John's" favourites, who said: "To be bored is to have failed in life"?

Lastly—and it is very important to remember it—there was always the kind heart behind the caustic word. After the explosion of fire and fury there was a quiet return to fairness; "I must *add*, of course...", he would say, in an altogether different tone. There is a story, well known in Kingston, of a young man who was to leave on one of those dismal 2 a.m. trains, to be married. The ring was not ready, and he had been asked by the jeweller to call for it on his way to the station. He hit the wrong house, rang and knocked. An angry red head appeared at an upper window, with "What's the matter?" "Mr Smith..." began the bridegroom. "Go to the devil!" was the instant rejoinder, followed by quick mollification and the courteous, but rather suggestive, words— "Next door."

§ 4. THE CLASS ROOM

My first approach to the University, which later became and still remains my most familiar one, was by the old side-gate on Arch Street. From this gate a narrow boardwalk led up the slope and turned past the residences to the East door of the Arts building. One recalls the distinctive smell of its worn and oiled softwood floors; the rows of varnished pine lockers along the walls; the dingy black cardboard signs, with their still dingier gilt lettering, that identified some of the lecture rooms and professors' rooms.

After some difficulty the Registrar's office was found. The entrance to it was under the landing of the stairs that led past the door of the gallery of Convocation Hall and on up to the top floor. The Registrar's office was an appalling little den—a spot straight out of a Dickens novel! How "G. Y." and his aide (I think the singular form is right), how they "got away with" working there, I still wonder. But why should the Registrar complain, when the Principal had no office at all? In later years, when the Registrar's department was in what to me will always be Dr Watson's classroom, a visitor was looking for Professor E. F. Scott, who then lived next to the Principal's House. "Is your father at home?" he asked the small daughter playing outside. "No, I think he's over in Mr Chown's College" was the reply.

In my day we climbed to the top floor for our Classics and Moderns. The plastered walls, of corridor and rooms alike, were innocent of paint. They had never been painted, but they bore countless signatures of our predecessors, so many in fact that except for a long-armed giant it was impossible to "sign on" without climbing on a window-sill or a bench.

A. B. Nicholson or "Little Nicky", as he was affectionately called, did his best for us in Classics. It is pleasant to recall his quick light step, the huge bushy eyebrows, the long gown, the glasses continually being put on and taken off again. He used to breathe fire against evildoers—one incident I recall vividly, that of "Kelly's Key". "Nicky" pounced on it and held it high. "I've been wasting my life—here it is all done for me"—and he read out some samples of Kelly's English style, and followed them with playfully serious advice against the use of a "crib".

Junior "Pheesics" was one of the bright spots. The glass rod that was rubbed with a bit of fur (with subdued "miaows" from the back benches) and then picked up bits of paper—the machine that stored up static electricity as "Davie" turned the crank, and the holding of hands round the room to take the shock from it—a later professor described these "properties" as having been rescued from Noah's Ark. "Thirty-two gram tachs per second per second"—the distinction between mass and weight illustrated by a hammer at rest and striking mock blows, and by the theoretical swinging of a heavy door, "if the heenges be trruly vairtical and well oiled, a small child may move it, though slowly". One just mugged up the text-book and got the class off, but the lectures were fun!

The Physics classes, Junior and Senior, were asked in groups of six or eight at a time to high tea at the professor's. Cynics said that one could not get out of the third division in the examination, without turning up. Be that as it may, the parties were unique. In fine weather one might be taken to the roof of the house to look through the telescope, more often you were shown Japanese curios. After high tea there were "prayers"; both the reading and the prayers were from the host's own book, a compilation of short selections from the sages. After each one the author was named—Confucius, Savonarola, the prophet Amos, Marcus Aurelius, John Bunyan, Ignatius Loyola...it was a truly catholic collection.

Senior Philosophy was, I think, the only class that was always opened with the reading of a prayer. This was a link between the early days of Queen's and the Universities of Scotland, where in John Watson's time the first lecture of the morning was prefaced with prayer. I enjoyed John Watson's class more than any other at Queen's. There was always the feeling of something unattainable yet worth trying to reach—the feeling that Watson was, as Wordsworth said of Newton,

forever
Voyaging through strange seas of Thought, alone.

Well, perhaps he was not actually always alone, but few of us shipped with him except on his shorter voyages. Even on these, however, one got an inkling of what philosophical thought might mean and a stimulus to seek for the underlying meaning in life, to refuse opinions at second or third hand, and, as St Paul said, to "examine all things".

Nathan Dupuis was a great teacher of mathematics—for the right kind of student. I was not of the elect; mathematics always left me "faint yet pursuing", and never catching up. I gave up the pursuit, but the mental panic of an Honours examination in mathematics still remains one of the major horrors of my youth. Dupuis' lectures are a pleasant enough memory—his lucid demonstrations on the blackboard, the tramping applause as he made his point or drew one of his perfect freehand circles, his odd pronunciation of the Greek letters used as symbols—Alphy, Sigmy, Thety, he called them. He perhaps excelled as a teacher in part because he was an expert craftsman: he had on his ancient push-bike the first cyclometer ever seen in Kingston—to the question "Where did you get it?" his reply was "I made it". "Nathan" despised heartily all inexact learning; he was dubious about Classics and Literature; his whole being, even his physical frame, was steeped in his own science—his characteristic

stoop, men said, was the result of overmuch digging for the
*n*th root of "Thety".

Somehow I always associated Adam Shortt with "the tutor,
the grave man Adam" in Clough's *Bothie*. Shortt's methods
were his own. His lectures were conversational and informal,
he broke new ground at Queen's by making his students
write serious essays on work allied to the lecture courses but
not directly part of them. He "got results", as the Americans
say; his students still swear by him. Among his Honours
men are the Professor of International Law at Harvard, the
Head of Economics at Williams College, a Director of the
Bank of England, the Deputy-Minister of External Affairs
at Ottawa, the Deputy-Minister of Education in Ontario.

Sir Wilfrid Laurier took Shortt from Queen's to be Head
of the Dominion Civil Service Commission, and from that
post he went to the Dominion Archives. Perhaps his greatest
work there was the securing of the Baring Papers for Canada.

Shortt was a self-taught wood-carver and sketcher in
pen-and-ink.

James Cappon, whether in the streets of Kingston with
his white bull-terrier Pete, or in his own lecture-room, was
the most Olympian of the senior men on the staff. He
appeared upon his little platform, he lectured—tramping up
and down in the trough he had worn in his little quarter-deck
—he gathered up his papers, he disappeared back into his
office. He seldom asked questions, and we had very little
writing to do, but "Cappy" was so burdened with lectures
that he could not have found time to read many essays. So
one had to get what he could from reading and lectures: it is
only fair to say that Cappon most certainly did set up
standards before us, by which to judge literature.

Senior Latin (Pass) was a new experience. For the first
time, the dry bones of a "dead" language were stirred;
instead of continually construing and parsing, we heard of a
Latin literature. (The truth of this, for it is true, is a sad

comment on the system one had been under. If the system had been less rigid, and more literary, Latin and Greek might to-day be more popular in Canada than they are.) Again and again, often within a very few moments after the class opened, formal questioning or construing ceased and we listened to a talk on ancient history, or classic art, or mythology, growing out of the Latin text. And the effect of it was not to decrease, but to increase, the amount of effort one was willing to make. To show us what could be done with a "dead" tongue, we were given prose exercises from the daily newspapers to work into Latin. Again, it was not enough to get the meaning of the Latin—it had to be put into idiomatic English. "Oh my dear sir—what an expression— I recommend to you the Authorized Version of the English Bible, it will improve your style."

The present generation can scarcely imagine the status of athletics in Queen's, thirty years ago. The cynical motto for the university of to-day, "Non Studium Sed Stadium", grows out of a newer soil. The rink was excellent, by the standard of the time (it was the best in Ontario, except that at Ottawa), but there was no "gym.", no stadium, no track. The track meet, in the autumn, was run off in the City Park, just east of Barrie Street. Rugby football practice was on the ground where the Douglas Library and Ontario Hall now stand, the dressing-rooms were in one corner of the cellar of the old frame "Tool House". The players provided most of their equipment; this was true also for hockey. Matches were played up at "The Athletic Grounds", where the city's tennis courts now are. It was a villainous field, with low spots which like the Psalmist's dry land became "pools of water"—occasionally they were deep enough to float a football when it fell in them. However, old Queen's held up well—in my four years she held the Senior Football championship once, the Intermediate twice, the Senior Hockey twice and "runner-up" honours twice.

§ 5. STUDENTS

From the class room we pass naturally to the students. From the first appearance of universities in the Middle Ages the students have been the real problem. The professor was there to teach them; in time there might be a permanent lecture-room—and then the university would cease to migrate; but what were you to do with the students out of the class room? How feed them, shelter them, control them, amuse them? Medieval Cambridge found landlady and grocer unsatis-factory, and devised the hostel kept (indeed for profit) by the academic person who taught his residents; and thence in a happy hour came the college. Medieval Paris and Aberdeen had their "nations". Queen's at Kingston started as a college; and so long as students were only to be reckoned by the dozen (and not many dozens), the problems of residence, discipline and amusement were all but negligible; but when the dozens grew to scores and to hundreds, and the college reached the numbers of a university, matters had to be thought over afresh. It is significant that it was the students who thought them out for themselves.

The essence of a college is that it is a society; so much is implied by the old Latin word which has no hint or suggestion of education about it; and a society implies some limitation of numbers. A university is also, strictly speaking, a society; but the modern university may be as desolate and depressing as the universe itself; only Stoics and cosmopolitans can be at home in the universe, because they alone need no home. Failing "colleges" in the English sense, without "residences", and not thinking of "nations", the students of Queen's grouped themselves in "years", the English word, for which "class" is the American. There was thus the "year ninety-nine"; and when the next crop of freshmen came it was decided they should be "noughty-nought", and they were. Students in

Theology hung together naturally, and were known as "divinities", and the Applied Science people were not yet too numerous to make a comfortable group, and they did not, yet, like their hungry generations, tread us down. So much for the smaller groups that made for friendship; athletics and other things were in the general charge of the Alma Mater Society; and discipline was entrusted to a *Concursus Iniquitatis et Virtutis*, a regular court, with chief justice, police and all, whose procedure was far more awful than its sentences. The sentences were mild enough; the procedure involved publicity and merciless wit; and the student never likes to be made ludicrous in public. So the *Concursus* was effective enough in a university of two up to five hundred or so students. Multiply the numbers by three or by four, and you will need new systems of grouping, and some new contrivances for discipline and athletics. The old machinery will hardly carry the new load; and so they are beginning to feel.

Yet quite recently the old-established Alma Mater Society achieved a real triumph. With the growth of numbers, and perhaps among them were men of more means, came the temptation to introduce the American fraternities—not the first adoption of American habits. Had not the professors more or less abandoned the Edinburgh model and (it proved, unhappily) recast their courses and their degree system on American lines? Had not the students tolerated the invasion of American "hazing" of freshmen—a babyish practice revealing at once the predominance of the unripe in American colleges and the flagrant poverty of American humour, in spite of Mark Twain and "the funnies"? Were not Mutt and Jeff, and Jiggs, debasing the national mind? So fraternities were to come in and to split the university with their inevitable snobbery. Then the Alma Mater Society acted; it would not have them; and no man should represent the university in athletics who belonged to a fraternity. None the less one was set up and enrolled some of the best of the football men. The Alma Mater stuck to its guns and refused to "play" them; Queen's should lose the inter-university championship first. The dread resolve was made; the "frat" man were not "played"; and the championship was won all the same.

But in our day we were not well-to-do enough to have fraternities, nor so undeveloped as to think "hazing" humorous or gentlemanly. Freshmen were encouraged (with the help of the *Concursus*) to avoid "cheek", though in England it is the "second year man" whom we dread; the Americans have their name for his spirit—it is "sophomoric". But we welcomed the freshmen with "receptions" in Convocation Hall and elsewhere. It gave them a chance to see girl students and civilization.

Of course it was a question what you should wear at such a "reception" or at the dances that in our period grew more frequent and more formal; and we witnessed the transition to dress clothes. This may seem odd enough to-day, when education is unthinkable without a dress suit; but it was given to us to see this $50 tax imposed upon every male student. (Heaven knows what girls' dresses cost then or cost now.) It was imposed, mark this! not by the college authorities, nor by the Alma Mater, but by that reluctance to be different, which begins when we go to our first school and haunts us to the tomb. It is the students, not the professors, who make education expensive; fees may now and then have to be raised, but it is social standards that cost. It may not be quite cynical to wonder how far they improve education; no doubt, they do contribute to a lad's development, but —well, we are in for dress-suits and "co-eds"; the one involved the other, and always has, from Eve's day. It was not all loss—far from it. To those accustomed to the "subfusc" decorum of the older universities, there was something of pain in the sight of a youth at Convocation coming forward to receive his medal, attired in a glaring yellow knicker suit under his gown—an unhappy cross between academic and demotic, if there was consolation in the thought that the medal was not for one of the real old studies but one of the more conjectural subjects nowadays supposed to be educative. Conversely the college was deeply moved when a charming Highlander from Prince Edward Island reappeared after a summer in Britain with a silk hat. It added something to the Sabbath to see him in it—the one silk hat of the university; one sees him still.

We all knew each other's business, as people do in family circles, and each other's Christian names. During examination time, when the piano was removed from the Convocation Hall to make room for papers and candidates, the boys used it freely in the intervals, and, when a certain professor appeared who was leaving for Britain to be married, they drifted somehow to "My Bonnie lies over the Ocean". When the poor lady christened Victoria received her degree, it was to the strains of the national anthem; what a lot we have to forgive our parents! How can they exercise such hideous ingenuity in giving a defenceless child a name that he can never live down? Convocation, when degrees honorary and ordinary were conferred, gave the humourist many chances. Thus once, when a new Catholic Archbishop, whose mother had been Highland if his father was French, came to the ceremony, and Principal Grant, not in his happiest vein, explained that "the Archbishop is like myself; he has some Scotch in him", a merciless wag sang out "So has Micky!" Every eye turned to the Honourable Irish Senator who lectured on Surgery, and the fact was evident. Lord Strathcona once came for an honorary degree; and, when it was conferred, and the parchment attesting it was being handed to him, a clear young voice was heard: "That'll just cost you twenty-five thousand dollars." "Geordie" impulsively started from his chair in sudden anger, and subsided. Queen's never received the money; but Lord Strathcona gave twice the sum to St John's, Cambridge. You can be too domestic in your manners.

Dean Inge once made a caustic criticism of Anglican seminaries for training clergy in small cathedral towns; what could be hoped when the gardeners were kept in greenhouses and the plants grew in the open? At Queen's everybody grew in the open, not least the Divinity students. Picture the training. Summer by summer the future parson might be working on a lake steamer, one year waiting at table, another lifting baggage, and later on he might be purser. The lake trip was a pleasant one (storms were not frequent) and to run the Lachine rapids was a sensation you would remember. The student was apt to find himself among a crowd recruited rather too much from the lower middle class of Rochester, N.Y., and adjoining American towns— frank vulgarians who nowadays enjoy the Hearst papers, and whose notion of a trip might (and often did) include devotions to Bacchus and Venus. The future parson was exposed to a very clear vision of his task and his field, of vulgar humanity unrestrained, unless the purser could control them. When he entered Divinity Hall, he would be pitchforked summer by summer into a prairie parish in the North West, where he must buy buggy and horse to cover his four hundred square miles of parish and see for himself how his Gospel affected the solitary farm-houses. Or it might be a mining camp with its peculiar types of men, and the women who went to mining camps. In the fall he came back to College, to study Theology with Grant and his colleagues, and perhaps Honour Philosophy with John Watson. Three or four winters in Arts, three winters in Theology, and the summers just described— they made the man or found him out; and the Presbyterians of Canada in those years had the strongest type of clergy to be met anywhere. There are of course people who never learn anything from experience or anything else; there were some of them no doubt in the ministry, but the training made for manhood.

It was a jolly college life that we knew—simple enough, gay too (for we all knew one another's eccentricities) and very friendly; and all this made for education. We did not produce many prigs; the atmosphere was against their growth—everybody knew everybody else too well to be imposed on; and that helped development. Truth, as Charles Lamb wrote to Wordsworth, should slide into the mind when it is imagining no such thing. Where friendship comes naturally and is instinctive, teacher and taught are on easier terms, there is no guarding oneself, and we give and take ideas, without realizing how much we are doing for one another. So it was in our class rooms; we knew all about one another and were prepared to find friends, and we did; and the class room, as we keep repeating in these pages, bred men and contributed to make "the Queen's spirit". The free handling of ideas, the incisive criticism only possible among friends, and the everlasting necessity to pull together achieved both these results. There was something Highland in Queen's from the start—Queen's grew to be a clan, and a clan, people tell us, we remain—perhaps alone among colleges we offered scholarships in Gaelic. Gaelic too, is *our* battle-cry, flung defiantly across the football field in victory or defeat, in fair weather or foul—

> OIL THIGH NA BANRIGHINN GU BRATH!
> CHA GHEILL! CHA GHEILL! CHA GHEILL!

But a clan, to be any good at all, must be a good clan.

Chapter VIII

G. M. GRANT

"Grant *is* Queen's"—so the newcomer was told; but, as Cicero would put it, "there is something in what you say, but not the whole story". But for Snodgrass and MacKerras Queen's would have ceased to be nine years before the date of Grant's coming (1877); yet it is not untrue to say that Grant made Queen's. It was not what the old divines called *creatio ex nihilo*, an act of sheer creation without pre-existent material. A story will make the thing clear. On one of his early campaigns in Ontario, when he was gathering endowments, Grant gave an address at Walkerton. Robert Sutherland, a lawyer more or less negro, of that town, had left "the first considerable bequest" to Queen's, a sum of about $11,000; and such an example, Grant felt, might stimulate others; but it hardly did. The chairman at his meeting gave $300, and the rest of the community did almost as much; Grant hoped on leaving that there might eventually be $1000 in all. But, whatever the total sum was, in his audience was a youth, who felt, as others felt when they met Grant, that he had never seen anybody like him; and the address so stirred him that he resolved not to go to Toronto University, as he had intended, but to Queen's, where this wonderful being was guiding the University; it must surely be more inspiring. So to Kingston he came in the following October; and the place and the college shocked him. However, as he had come, he would give it a trial; he would stick it out till Christmas—he was pretty tough in grain, to the end of life, this young man; and in January he would shift to Toronto. So he planned; but his stay at Queen's was thirty years or more. Grant had brought him to Queen's; Queen's kept him; there was something about the place, something of spirit, something in professors and students, that held Adam Shortt. Put in very vulgar phrase, Grant was a first-class drummer, but he travelled in a good article; and it got better and better under his care. If he "made" Queen's, he had capital building material; the place already had its distinctive personalities. The great trouble was financial.

Endowment campaigns—Snodgrass had started them; and Grant carried them on. Snodgrass was traditionally reported to have accepted a donation of fifty cents to endow the University. In those days the habit was not yet strongly established among millionaires of making huge gifts to colleges; for one thing Ontario was not yet producing millionaires in any great quantity; and Queen's had links with Presbyterianism—very curious links. It was neither the creation nor the property of either of the Presbyterian churches of Canada, nor of the church made in 1875 by their union. The church did not endow Queen's, but the connection always gave the excuse of "denominationalism" to people who wanted to escape from Grant. And then, as he observed —and his observations were always shrewd and could be caustic—every congregation and every town to which he went had "peculiar circumstances". But what Grant set his mind on was apt sooner or later to be achieved; his energy and enthusiasm, his geniality, swept obstacles away and made friends for the University wherever he went, in spite of themselves. It could not be said of him, as was said of another advocate, that he had the gift of creating an atmosphere of goodwill for Queen's, but somehow was unable to convert it into showers of blessing. But when academic persons take to raising money, somebody pays for it; "Queen's killed MacKerras", said Grant, "and has half-killed me."

Toward the end of Grant's life, in 1901, a proposal was

made, that the county of Frontenac, in which Kingston stands, should vote $50,000 toward a new building for Queen's. On this every owner of property in the county had a vote, and the proposal was opposed. The voters were largely farmers, for whom a dollar was a dollar and a serious consideration. Grant's attitude on Prohibition had not increased the number of his friends; and there were those who suspected (not unjustly) that the students might dance in the hall to be built with Frontenac money; education and immorality, it was too well known, went hand in hand. So the voting turned against Queen's College. But then the students came to the rescue, and decided themselves to raise the money; some of it they would give, taking so many years to complete their promises, the rest they would collect; the building, they stipulated, would be called Grant Hall—no other name. William Harty, the M.P., a Roman Catholic, came to their aid with $1000, he too stipulating that it should be Grant Hall. Such testimony of Queen's men at large cannot be mistaken or misconstrued; it meant the equation of Grant and Queen's.

But when we speak of Grant Hall, another benefactor deserves to be recalled, for various reasons. A Chinese laundryman had for some years advertised in the students' paper; and, perhaps only half-seriously, some of the students suggested to him that he should contribute to Grant Hall. He rose to it at once; no Chinese in the city should outdo him, he said; and Hong Lee contributed $50 in cash. It made a sensation, and his portrait was printed in the Toronto *Globe*. After that Hong Lee added another $100. Not a bad advertisement, some will say; but a more generous opinion was expressed by a man long resident in China and intimate with the people—the Chinese, he said, really believe in education. It is also pointed out that Grant had steadily stood out against the policy of excluding the Chinese from the Dominion.

§ 1. PICTOU COUNTY AND GLASGOW

In 1773 Dr Johnson and James Boswell made their famous tour in the Highlands. On 12 September they saw at Portree in Skye the ship *Nestor* taking Highland emigrants, driven by the lairds from their old homes, to the new world. Ten days later Boswell saw the *Margaret of Clyde*, similarly laden with Highland people for North America. Was it to Nova Scotia they were going? It was in that year, at all events, that Highland immigration began; and many followed the first settlers in a country reinforced with United Empire Loyalists. James Grant, whose forebears had long cultivated the little farm of Balnellan, where Avon and Spey meet in Banffshire, came out to Nova Scotia in 1826, aged twenty-five—to Pictou County, of course. It is remarkable always and everywhere how great a contribution of men Nova Scotia has made both to Canada and the States; there is something to be said for the dictum that "in the seventeenth century the pick of England went to New England; in the eighteenth the pick of New England went to Nova Scotia"; and, when you begin to be more precise, Pictou County is sure to be mentioned by some one. James Grant married in 1831 a woman from Inverness, Mary Monro, of godly lineage and godly character; and George Monro Grant, born 22 December 1835 (the day before his father's birthday) was their third child.

James Grant, like many another immigrant, made no great success of his life in the New World, if you measure by dollars. He was schoolmaster, farmer, auctioneer, amateur lawyer, a friendly figure, and rather too ready at "putting his hand to paper" for his friends to be able to amass much of what he did earn. In one of his farming periods a new invention was installed at the pithead of a neighbouring mine—a hay-cutter. Among those who inspected it was George Monro Grant, aged seven; and it was like the Grant

Plate XII

Photo: Notman

G. M. Grant

we all knew that he must experiment with it. The older people had turned their backs, and the small boys began to chop hay, when a sudden cry brought the men back. The boy's hand was sliced off just below the thumb. He was carried off home, a small friend running alongside and saying, "Dinna greet, Geordie; I hae the fingers". But Geordie never had them again. To the end he wore on the right hand an odd-shaped glove with a little pocket in it, and with this and the one joint of the thumb that was left he did wonders. But the left hand was all he had to write with; and most of his friends will associate his greeting at once with a genial smile and the outstretched left hand.

It was clear that Geordie would hardly be a farmer now, but no one who knew the man could have imagined that any farm would content him; he was built for wider activities, and he found them. It is not needful here to give precise detail about school and church and home in Nova Scotia. There was schooling—there always would be where Scottish parents were concerned; and there were churches and controversies, linked up with those of Scotland, to stimulate thought about religion and churchmanship. Burghers and Anti-Burghers—how little Canada remembers of them; but controversy quickens intelligence, where there is intelligence, and children of brains grow up better where argument is a major part of life. Later on Grant decided, with Norman MacLeod, that for the religious welfare of a community an established church was best, surrounded by a vigorous dissent. Freedom of discussion and freedom of mind—they are part of the true Scottish endowment, and they were part of Grant's ideal for a free country; but he was not for multiplication of small sects—it must be *vigorous* dissent to be any good. Both his parents were Scots, and from the Old Country; and they brought the heritage of Scottish song and Scottish story, and the boy entered into it. One outstanding

160 *G. M. Grant*

memory of Grant at sixty is the sight of him in the Senate Room at Queen's, after lecture, deeply immersed in Neil Munro's story *John Splendid*, then appearing month by month in *Blackwood's*. That was the real Highland stuff, he and his brother-Scots decreed.

It was fortunate for Grant, and for his life-work and his friends, that means were found by some church bursary to send him to Glasgow University. It is good for the Canadian-born to live for years in the Old Country, as it is for the Old Country man to live for years in Canada—to realize that there are at least two ways of life, both right ways, and two traditions both of high value. The original homeland is never the same afterwards; there is always contrast, and contrast liberates. Grant knew Nova Scotia, and he now came to know Scotland. Later on, in two great journeys to the Pacific, surveying with Sandford Fleming, he was to learn his Canada, as no one learns it now. His canvasses of Ontario revealed that province to him, as his great holiday journey to Australia and Cape brought new aspects of the Empire under his survey—yes, and "into his business and bosom". Point by point, all his experience was of the kind that enlarges range and gives freedom of mind.

It was not the college on Gilmore Hill that Grant knew, the Gilbert Scott building, high above the Kelvin and recalling the Parliament House over the Ottawa. Gilmore Hill is the higher, but the Ottawa is a brighter sight than the Kelvin. The pilgrim from Queen's will not readily find the scene of Grant's lectures, debates, arguments, orations and football triumphs. He was once arrested on a charge of stabbing a fellow-student; there was no knife, but a fist had been used, and blood drawn, in defending a small man from a big in a snowball fight; and the Glasgow magistrate dismissed the charge with a compliment to Grant, followed by cheers from a concourse of students, cheers for Grant and for the Bailie. He lived thriftily; that was his upbringing, and to the end everybody at Queen's knew how careful he was of the dollars, and how he had "a horror of waste", domestic or national. It would have been good for the North West provinces if they had had more of his spirit. He was deeply interested in the slum-life of Glasgow, but he knew the countryside too. He tramped over Scotland, which is the real way to know a land so full of beauty and of legend. He also saw something of the continent, particularly Luther's country. He "sat under" the great preachers of Scotland, who showed him what real preaching was; he might criticize them, but Liddon, he felt, fell very far short of the Scotsmen he had known. At last he was ordained to what was called a *vagum ministerium*—which does not mean vague, as a colleague wickedly suggested. He returned to Nova Scotia in 1860, with the encomium of Norman MacLeod to the effect that, if he did not speak Gaelic, "he would back his friend, Mr Grant, against any man for speaking in the English language". Dr MacLeod was right; so many of us found.

§ 2. IN HALIFAX

To his ministry in Nova Scotia only a few words can be given here. He came back to his province no provincial, but a man of ideas, who had been living in the world, with a new vista of national history behind him, a new consciousness of Europe, and a new outlook on things Biblical and Theological. One would hardly at any time have called Grant a scholar, in the technical sense; but perhaps for the work he was called upon to do, as minister in Halifax and as lecturer at Queen's, he was the more useful for not being a scholar. It is forgotten sometimes that immense learning, or even brilliant originality in handling the texts of an ancient literature, is only a very partial endowment. "Knowledge

comes, but wisdom lingers"; and there is a place, very em-
phatically there is, in church and university life for the man
who understands scholarship, who sympathizes with what the
scholar does, and brings to bear on scholar and scholarship
a criticism founded on life and enlarged by range of experience. But he must understand the scholar's mind and
realize the significance of his work, or his criticism will be of
no value. Grant sooner or later got a good grasp of what
scholarship was doing; and he was gifted with a faculty for
making other men realize it, for setting the door open—in
short, in this as in much of his other work, his function was
the splendid one of offering men the opportunity of a larger
life and inspiring them to embark on it.

In Nova Scotia he bore his part also in the discussions that
brought about the union of Presbyterian churches. It was
something to have known from childhood the arguments
and the atmosphere of Burghers and Anti-Burghers, and in
early manhood to have lived the life of Presbyterian Scotland
and seen the old small-town rivalries from a distance. A
sense of range, if one may repeat, marked all Grant's outlooks;
he belonged to what we used to call "the great open spaces".
Beside the future of the church, he had to think of education,
and particularly university education; but as Dalhousie is
not in our Corner of Empire, we must not digress to that
university. Two things should be noted, however. Grant
came to Queen's with a considerable experience of university
life and university problems. Glasgow was made already,
with centuries of European tradition; Dalhousie was in the
making; and both opened the man's mind—to values and
to questions. He knew more about these things, when he was
plunged into the university controversies of Ontario, than
some of the people who handled them. "I have no faith in
second-rate universities", he said in 1895.

He became a preacher, but not (to judge from later years)

of the type that deals much in unction (whatever that is) or emotion. Perhaps he would have been a greater preacher if he could have allowed his listeners to divine something more of the emotion that he really felt. He used to tell of an Irish saloon-keeper of notorious character in Halifax, who came up to him with a beaming face after a service. "A grand sermon, Mr Grant", he said, "a grand sermon; it did me good to listen to it." Grant was surprised; "I rather thought", he rejoined, "that some parts of it hit you rather hard." "My dear fellow", said the Irishman, putting an affectionate hand on Grant's shoulder, "it's a poor sermon that doesn't hit me somewhere."

It was while he was still living in Halifax in 1872 that Grant made his first great expedition with Sandford Fleming to the Pacific, in preparation of the plans for the route of the Canadian Pacific Railway. Grant was tremendously keen on this project; it was pledged to British Columbia as the price of entry into Confederation. Grant had always believed in the union of Canada, and insisted on the Dominion fulfilling its bargain with the remote province which the Queen had named. He wrote the story of the journey, an interesting travel record in any case, and by now a "scarce" book, a "document" in the history of Western Canada. A very human sort of book it is too, and a joyful book. Grant had to rough it with the men, riding, rain-drenched, weary, day after day, over prairie and torrent, burnt lands and mountains; but this did not worry him; throughout life he gave the impression of not caring about any high standard of comfort. The dominant note of the book is exultation in the glorious land he was surveying and the great future it was bound to know. The air, the soil, the climate, the prospects —some day, he said, it would be exporting 20,000,000 bushels of wheat in a year—a prophecy men called ridiculous; he lived to see the figure reach 55,000,000 bushels. "A fair land;

rich in furs and fish, in treasures of the forest, the field, and the mine; seamed by navigable rivers, interlaced by numerous creeks, and beautified with a thousand lakes; broken by swelling uplands, wooded hillsides, and protected on its exposed sides by a great desert or by giant mountains. The air is pure, dry, and bracing all the year round; giving promise of health and strength of body and length of days." But, as he said, "a nation is saved by ideas, inspiring and formative ideas"; and he dwelt on the happiness which the great land would mean to millions, and the strength it would give to the Empire. But somehow one feels that, quite apart from geology and climate and empire, Grant thoroughly enjoyed the adventure with his friend. At any rate he went a second time over the ground with him; for when the Yellow Head Pass was given up, and Sandford Fleming wished to see for himself the wonderful Kicking Horse Gorge (fifty miles as it were of the Pass of Killiecrankie, a fierce stream between towering mountains), Grant was again his companion. It must be a matter of regret to many who worked with him or under him at Queen's that his book was not more familiar, and that they did not know him in his character of pioneer. He had "stared at the Pacific" and seen the future; and he was the man who could use experience. The opportunity was not long in coming; the "young lion" of Halifax was called to Ontario and to Queen's, and he came. It was his life-work at last, and the forty-two years of training all found their use.

§ 3. AT QUEEN'S

So Grant came to Queen's; and it is of interest, not merely local, to see what he came to, and what he brought with him.

The nadir for the University had been in December 1868, when, as surviving freshmen of that year have told us, it was doubtful whether there would be any college for them at all when they returned from the Christmas vacation. Snodgrass, the Principal, and MacKerras, Professor of Classics, as we have seen, saved the University. It must also be remembered, and it is significant that, even when things were at the worst, the students held by the college—unlike the students at Cobourg. So early was what is known as the "Queen's spirit" a factor in our affairs. The tide had turned but it had not flowed far. There were still perils; but there were students who meant to stay, and there were professors. Watson and Dupuis were there—personalities both of them (if we may use hackneyed language), very different types, but each "a definite effect"; and they taught for a full generation more. Queen's had a site, too, and it was not long before Grant and his trustees by a wise purchase enlarged the Campus to its present extent.

But let us look at what Grant brought to Queen's—and it was what she eminently needed and as eminently welcomed. He brought youth, energy, outlook, inspiration. "We at Queen's believe in ideas", he said to a man he wished to secure as a colleague. He had believed in the union of the Presbyterian churches, in the Confederation of the Dominion, in the linking of Atlantic and Pacific; he understood what oceans meant in the world, and he thought in terms of a continent. He believed in Canada—every way—from ocean to ocean, her past in Frenchman and Scot and Loyalist, her future; and his faith in his country was an inspiration to other men; it never flagged, it was never concealed; and it meant that nothing little, nothing mean, nothing dirty, should for him ever be associated with the name of Canada. Politicians are—politicians; and men said that Grant could "play politics" with the best of them; but he thought of his country and her place in the world, her place in the future, as a statesman, whose interest was in the ideal not in the dodge. Sir John Macdonald himself was the Member of

Parliament for Kingston, and brother-in-law of Grant's quaint old colleague Dr Williamson; and they met in the Professor's house. "How I wish, Principal Grant", said Sir John, "that you would be a steady friend of mine." "Why, Sir John, I have always supported you when you were right." Sir John's eyes twinkled. "My dear man", he said, "I have no use for that species of friendship." It was all that Grant would give to any of them, and it won him a position in Dominion affairs that no other man had—above party, but no doctrinaire, a man of ideas and principles, who could very conspicuously take a part in public and political life without compromise on the great issues of country and honesty. Little as we then may have thought about it amid the ups and downs of college life, it was yet no small part of the education that Queen's gave to associate with a man of such outlooks, such range and such political integrity. As the years pass, the man grows in stature.

If there was nothing small in his conception of Canada, Canada was yet a part of a larger organism, the Empire. Grant was one of the pioneers among the Imperialists, who changed the suggestion of the word from acquisition of subject lands to the practical federation of sister-nations. If the Canadian Pacific Railway was, as Grant always insisted, essential for Canada's existence, an integral part of Canada, it was no less an artery of the Empire at large, an immense contribution to the unity of Greater Britain made by the oldest Dominion. To many of us, Canadian-born or from Britain, the idea was new; and once again it was part of our education to have the larger outlook brought inevitably before us by a man of Grant's power and vision. Empire? He knew far more of Empire than any of us did—*knew* more, and believed more. "We at Queen's believe in ideas", and whatever the provincial and the parochial say, it is the great idea, the broad range, that wins the young and makes them over again. To set men at a universal point of view, was Watson's account of the function of a university; and Grant's contribution to this was very great. In those days Goldwin Smith, the Oxford historian, was in Toronto, croaking for ever that Canada's only future lay in her dissolution and piecemeal absorption as so many disconnected "states" into the American republic. Some of us will forgive Goldwin Smith a good deal for his share in Conington's *Virgil* and his exquisitely written short history of the United States; but he takes some forgiving. Grant stood up against all *that* talk, for a United Empire; and after forty years his conception, the wider ideal, is in the ascendant. Bad years and good, imperial crises, world-disasters, and hard-won victory have lifted us all together, forward.

For the University, as we have seen, Grant cherished high ideals—he had "no faith in second-rate universities". There are peculiar perils, quite other than financial perils that beset places of learning. There is the very idea of learning which is unexpectedly a peril; so many students, and alas! so many professors, cannot get rid of the notion that education is merely the Latin for "learning things". We knew that type in Queen's—the student who learnt his books by heart, and the professor who could only "cram" and had no idea of liberating the mind. Own brothers to them both is the advocate of the trade-school; that heresy which nowadays in sheer shame he calls "vocational training"; how valuable, he says, to train the youth to do exactly what he will spend his life in doing. Grant never believed in this kind of stuff, and the stronger part of his staff were with him. "The universal point of view" was their ideal—neither cramming, nor coaching. We had no school of business, no department of brewing, no "school of pedagogy" (word and thing beloved of prigs and officials); all we sought to do was to train *men* (including women, of course, from 1878), to give them outlook, to encourage thought and insight, gifts fit for every kind of life, needful if a man is to be human of the highest quality. An ideal high enough! but the only one for a university; and, in spite of textbooks and their adherents, Queen's stood for this ideal. She did not owe it entirely to Grant: the men he found there had it; but what would have become of them and their ideal, if Grant had been the other sort? And the other sort appeals so much to practical mothers and hack officials and dull lads; and Ontario, like other English lands, knew all these sad types. Teacher, builder, driver—call Grant what you will; he saved the University from intellectual ruin as surely as he did from financial; and, with all his limitations, his presence, his word, his glance, were inspiration.

There is another peril which he helped us to escape. Universities can become denationalized, schools of research, where Physics, Chemistry and the like are pursued to the utmost, and culture, manhood and citizenship are atrophied and die out. But the spirit of Queen's was national; it could be nothing else with Grant at the helm, and the strong group around him.

§ 4. GRANT THE MAN

Grant had limitations, and serious ones. Boswell said about his *Life of Johnson* that he "would not make his tiger a cat for any one". Grant's weak points then have to be considered. After all, knowledge of a great man's weaknesses and bad qualities does not necessarily lower our estimate of him; it forces us to grasp how strong his better gifts must have been to outweigh the faults, to enable him in spite of himself to achieve what he did. There was a ruthlessness about Grant, very apt to be found in men of high ideals. General Booth once stayed with Grant; and Grant would laughingly tell how disillusioned his old servant, an ardent Salvation Army soldier, was by Booth's abrupt dismissal of her to get tea for him; she even began to prefer the Principal—poor soul! Grant could treat his own followers and supporters in the same way. Indeed, it was said, bitterly, that "Grant has no friends; for when he is through with a man, he shakes him". This was not without some truth. Grant was devoted to his wife; his tenderness and affection for her come out in the letters that their son printed, and she deserved it. But this kind of thing happened. Some proposal was before the Queen's Senate (the body of Professors), not to be settled quite offhand; should it be printed and circulated? How much would it cost? asked Grant. About a dollar. "Then Mrs Grant will type it." And she did. She too had to subserve the cause of Queen's, and she was no doubt glad to do it. And so he was apt to treat everybody else.

He sacrificed himself ruthlessly for Queen's, picked his own pocket (as it were) for the college, and came (it seemed) to think he had a right to pick everybody else's pocket round the place, for the one cause which they all supported, and in which they all believed. There are different ways of picking a man's pocket; increased work, a heavy increase, without a cent more of salary seemed to some men rather like robbery, when they were told they could go, if they didn't like it— Grant knowing, as they knew, that there was nowhere for them to go, that they were at his mercy. Increase of salary? Not a bit of it! "Every tub stands on its own bottom", he would say; "why, I ——". He said "why I ——" too often, and did not realize, or chose not to realize, that to tell an obscure colleague, "why, I, when I want more money, I write an article for fifty dollars", was mockery. Who would buy *their* articles for fifty dollars, or for five? He was a public figure; they were not. He had always some sophistry to justify a manœuvre by which a colleague was mulcted somehow—always for the benefit of Queen's. Yet straighter dealing with those colleagues would have produced as much for the college, and without the taste that his cleverness sometimes left.

He could be rough with the uncouthness of a peasant, grossly rude in anger, speaking to give pain. His son speaks of his hot temper, quoting a beautiful letter to Mrs Grant, written from the other side of the world; and says that, after that great holiday (his only real one) and the younger boy's death, the temper never flared at home in the old way. But he met his match now and then. "Professor McBlank", he said, with malice prepense, for he was angry with the man; "I hear you didn't lecture on Tuesday." "No, Principal", rejoined the Irishman; "I was going to, but I heard of the death of the Queen, and after that I could not lecture." "Ah, but, Professor McBlank, we can't have individual professors doing that sort of thing; we must act together; Queen's is an organism." "And I too, Principal", returned the colleague, "am an organism."

But it was always for the cause of Queen's. From the early days in Halifax he had been contemptuous of appeals to his own interest. Some one, possibly with the best intentions, when Grant moved house, had a new carpet laid for him; Grant asked to have it removed—"I am your clergyman and in that capacity I may some day have a delicate task to perform. No carpet or other article of furniture shall rise between me and my duty." This may have been excessive scrupulosity, but it was not self-seeking. In his Ontario days, when he was a great public figure, it was the same; he would not accept passes from the railways. He was invited to become Minister of Education in Ontario, and he declined the invitation. It was suggested that, if Queen's would move to Toronto and sink herself there, he should be Principal of the combined university. But he chose to stay at Queen's, on a salary of $3000; and how many people nibbled at that, nobody knows. Needy students were helped; one looked after his furnace; one after another lived in his house. Sometimes they told him tales out of school, to which in his later days he paid more attention than he need have. But there the man was, with great qualities, and the defects of his qualities, greater than those before him and than those who came after him.

If contemporary evidence for a great character and its foibles is desired, a verse from a student song supplies it—

Does you know the famous George Monro, de leader of de band?
     Chorus We does!
Does you b'lieve dere ain't his equal in dis or any land?
     Chorus We does!
Does you know how he will lub you when he wants your little pile?
Does you always run to meet him when he wears that pleasant smile?

Of his inner life he was not apt to speak, but his son prints letters which reveal what others never saw. The man who penned the sentence that the Gospel is redemption as well as revelation, must have been near the heart of the matter. Looking back across thirty years and more, clear away from the small frictions and diplomacies of college life, one sees that Grant was bigger than he sometimes showed himself. He had real convictions; he did believe in truth; he believed in the mind and its right to freedom. He had great gifts, and he dedicated them to a great cause; Queen's had a sacred purpose, or it was nothing; it should be, he determined, a real centre of opportunity, where those, who would, and who were fit for it, should find an open door to all truth—an entry into the fullest life, a vision, a universal point of view, that should change their outlook, as Cicero's *Hortensius* changed all the thoughts of St Augustine, and set them, like that great saint, on fire to know the highest things and the best. As long as this is our ideal at Queen's, Grant's work will live; there is no fear about that.

INDEX

For EU product safety concerns, contact us at Calle de José Abascal, 56–1°,
28003 Madrid, Spain or eugpsr@cambridge.org.

www.ingramcontent.com/pod-product-compliance
Ingram Content Group UK Ltd.
Pitfield, Milton Keynes, MK11 3LW, UK
UKHW012347130625
459647UK00009B/591